To my parents for creating me – in all senses of the word. To my editor, Jon Finch, for giving me the opportunity to stretch my wings with Kogan Page. To my colleagues at Kiddy and Partners for keeping me grounded with their humour and supporting me in my writing endeavours alongside my consulting work. Special thanks to Brian Baxter for reading the draft and making constructive suggestions. And to Steve Cuthbertson for bringing me Swiss chocolates to fuel late night writing sessions.

Contents

Introduction

I saw an advertising slogan for a recruitment agency a few years ago that said, 'The job for life is dead. Long live jobs for life.' I thought that it summed up very succinctly what many business school professors, sociologists and other commentators in the world of work have been saying for a few years now. Gone are the days when you could expect your employer to look after you. Only a few decades ago, you could join an employer after leaving school or university and wait for your employer to provide training for you, determine your career path, and give you occasional pay rises and promotions for the length of your career. The psychological contract between employer and employee implicitly assumed that employees would work hard and be loyal to their employer in return for the employer providing work for life. But that is no longer the case.

The world of work is changing. What with globalization and increasing pressure to perform, organizations have been engaging in downsizing, delayering, and even 'right-sizing'. As a result no job can be guaranteed for life. The old hierarchies are getting stripped away in an effort to reduce cost, and with fewer layers there can only be fewer opportunities for promotion. And even though you may be able to find some sort of job for yourself, will it be as challenging and satisfying as it should be? The message is that if you do not take steps to look after yourself, your employer is not going to do it for you.

The psychological contract between employer and employee has changed, and this book recognizes that fact. The psychological contract for the 21st century assumes that employees will take the responsibility for managing their own careers. So individuals must search the world of work for employers who will offer them the opportunity to pick up new skills and experiences that will make them employable for the future.

Unfortunately, the world of work can be a perilous place without an employer looking out for you. However, this is exactly the sort of work that – as business psychologists – my colleagues and I do on a day-to-day basis. We work with all sorts of individuals and teams of people as well in a variety of organizations in industries ranging from publishing to construction, and consumer goods to investment banking. But, recognizing that we cannot meet all of our potential audience in person, this book sets out to help you look after yourself: tackling the issues that we have most frequently come across in recent years.

Not sure whether you are in the right job or not? Not sure whether you have spent too long working for the one employer? Or maybe you are wondering how to beat off competition from your peers and climb the career ladder? If any of these questions describe you, then this is the book for you. These are just some of the other career questions that this book sets out to help you answer:

- How can I get the promotion I think I deserve?
- Am I really happy doing what I am doing at the moment?
- How can I juggle my personal goals and aspirations with my need to earn a living?
- I find myself unemployed: how can I find a new and satisfying job?
- How can I be happier and more successful in my current job?
- How can I find a different employer who will value me (and pay me) more?
- What can I do to improve my career prospects?
- How can I have a career and not just a job?

The good news is that most people have not realized that they need to take their careers into their own hands. Or, if they have realized, they are too lazy to do anything about it. So for the minority of people such as you, the reader, who is willing to invest in thinking about your career, you will be able to carve out a successful and rewarding career.

PUTTING IN THE HARD WORK

There is no magic formula to achieving a better career, I am afraid. You cannot simply wave a magic wand and hope to have a more successful and satisfying career in a few easy steps. You cannot simply read the book from start to finish and expect your new life to appear. In fact, any book that claims instant results is trying to pull the wool over your eyes. It is going to take hard work.

I would recommend strongly that you do not read this book all in one go. There are many exercises and questionnaires for you to complete, contemplate, and come back to. You may read a section, go have a coffee, start an exercise and leave it for a week before finishing it. You might then need to take a few days to talk the implications over with colleagues, friends or other confidantes. Advice that is written in a book can never provide you with all of the answers, especially when it concerns something as momentous as your work and life. This book is only meant to stimulate your thinking and give you a handful of ideas: but you need to invest the time, thought and energy to reflect on how those ideas could help you in achieving your personal career goals.

But this book is not just about analysis and logical thinking to determine what you should be doing in the future. Your feelings and intuition have an important part to play in helping you to get the most out of this book. There are quizzes and exercises in here that are designed to make you think, but they are not aimed at pushing you in one career direction over another. The ultimate test of whether a career decision is right for you is whether you feel that it is the right thing for you. For some people then, the hard work comes in using their intuition and tapping into their feelings as much as using logic and planning.

The hard work does not stop there. You may need to challenge beliefs and assumptions you hold about yourself or have to face uncomfortable truths. You may have to address interpersonal issues at work, training or retraining may be necessary, and maybe you will need to spend evenings and weekends studying. And it is certain to take months rather than days or weeks to see any real improvement in the quality of your working life. However, if you stick with it, this book will put you on the right course to having a more enjoyable and profitable career.

HOW TO USE THIS BOOK

This book is designed for you to skip around. I recommend that you start with Chapter 1 because this involves the most thinking on your part and you really need to have a good idea of what you want to achieve in your life (both in and out of work) before you start wading into the advice sections in later chapters.

Once you have read Chapter 1, however, you may want to jump to whatever interests you the most. This book sets out to guide you through some of the most common career dilemmas that people face. The issues that we face in our work do not crop up in a linear fashion: your career is not a journey that follows a predetermined path. Consequently, there is no reason why you should read this book in a linear fashion either. Skip around from chapter to chapter to whatever you need to read for where you are in your career. Having said that though, the chapters are broadly split into three sections:

Doing what you do but better

Perhaps you are happy at the moment to stay in your chosen career and to continue working for your current employer. But perhaps you want more. If you are sick of seeing less talented but more political colleagues succeed ahead of you, then Chapter 2 will help you to identify politicking and prevent people from getting the better of you. But while the motives of the office politician may be wrong, the skills they sometimes use to influence and persuade others can be put to ethical use for you; a topic that is handled in Chapter 3. After all, we can all probably think of examples of people who have succeeded in the workplace not because they are the brightest or most skilled person, but because they are the best connected and most influential.

Having said that though, it is sometimes the case that individuals stagnate and do not do enough to boost their skills and employability. Chapter 4 should give you some ideas about the kinds of skills that will help you to get ahead. Chapter 5 outlines some of the (sometimes tedious) hoops – appraisals, internal interviews and assessments – that we may have to jump through to get ahead at work. Chapter 6 may help you to think about some of the leadership challenges you may face, should you wish to take on the responsibilities of becoming a manager.

Sometimes, it is not our skills or the lack of them that holds us back: but other people's *perceptions* of whether we have those skills or not. Chapter 7 should help you to figure out how you come across to others and how to improve your impact on them.

Handling career dissatisfaction

Chapter 8 tries to tackle an increasing issue for many people. Many of us feel compelled to work harder and for longer hours to fend off competitive colleagues. As a consequence, our work is increasingly encroaching on our personal lives. This chapter will help you to think about how to address the balance between your working life and personal life.

Chapter 9 offers more practical advice on tackling possible imbalances between your work and personal life. If you are working hard, you may feel that you deserve greater rewards for your efforts. Or, you may decide to renegotiate your working hours to better suit your personal needs.

Changing direction

Chapters 10–12 offer thoughts and advice on changing jobs. But there is no advice here on mere interview skills. These chapters challenge you to think about whether you are doing work that really satisfies your interests and personal needs.

Chapter 10 asks you to think about whether you are in the right job, and what sort of work environment and culture you should be looking for in your next job.

Responding to job adverts is old hat. The new way to find a better job is covered in Chapter 11. And finally, when you think that you may have found the right job for you, Chapter 12 provides you with some thoughts and checklists to ensure that it really will be as perfect as it should be.

So keep this book with you on the lifetime journey of your career. Let me know how it goes!

Rob Yeung
robyeung@robyeung.freeserve.co.uk

1

Establishing your values and career priorities

Surveys repeatedly show that most people are not entirely happy with their jobs. Certainly, most people can explain some of the reasons why they are unhappy with their current job: perhaps it's the long hours, too much stress, or too little excitement. Oddly enough though, very few people can really describe what their ideal, but realistic (we are not talking about being paid for sipping cocktails while lying on a beach somewhere exotic!) job would be.

We all recognize that working just for the sake of money is not that rewarding. Of course, we would all like to get paid more for what we do: but that is not the solution in itself. People are increasingly asking themselves what really motivates them. Do you want to be known for your achievements at work or your achievements outside of work? Putting it another way, do you want to be measured in terms of your work success or in terms of your life's significance?

Perhaps it's time for you to read on and think about what you really want out of your life and therefore where your career should be headed. This chapter contains a series of self-test questionnaires and exercises to help you think about your personal likes and dislikes, your priorities and values: all of which will help you to be happier and more successful in your chosen career.

A WARNING

Most people dislike taking time to think about themselves. The vast majority of people like to act as opposed to think. In thinking about themselves, most people would rather be given a series of questionnaires that gives them answers on a plate, whereas the exercises in this chapter mainly require you to sit down and engage in some quiet thinking. And it is hard work too, thinking about yourself and really thinking about what you want out of your life and career.

When I work with individuals, they often say that they do not have the time to do the exercises in this chapter. They say that they already know what they want out of their lives and their careers: they just want help in achieving it. They want something that they can act upon, as opposed to taking time to think and reflect. However, it is usually the individuals who do take this initial time out to reflect and think about their goals and aspirations who actually get the most out of the rest of the chapters of this book.

You have been warned. If you want to get the most out of this book, you need to spend at least a couple of good hours completing the exercises in this chapter first.

UNDERSTANDING THE IMPORTANCE OF CORE VALUES

We are much more likely to succeed in our careers when we are doing something that we value. It may sound obvious, but you would be amazed at the number of people who spend years or even decades slogging away at a job that does not motivate them, simply because they have never sat down and really thought about what they value.

However, we all have different values. One person may be motivated by the thrill of running a big business, while another individual might be driven by the thought of running a local business that makes a difference to their local community. Another person may put personal and spiritual growth above all else. Yet another may seek predictable working hours that will allow him or her to put family above work interests.

Distilling our values helps us to focus. The benefits of spending time on working out your *personal* values include:

- You will be much more likely to succeed in your chosen career if you are doing work that you believe in.

- You will have a clear direction for not only your career but also your life. Whenever you are faced with an important decision, you will be able to choose what is best for you in the long run rather than what may be the most initially enticing. For example, it is easy to be tempted into new jobs because they offer a bigger salary: but how compatible is that with your goals in life?

- You will be able to achieve not only success, but also satisfaction from your professional life.

A final warning before we begin with the first exercise. A lot of big businesses have corporate visions, mission statements and values statements that try to encapsulate what makes them different. These corporate statements are supposed to motivate employees – but in practice few of them make any difference at all. Most employees would be hard pressed to quote their corporate values – and the reason is because all of these vision, mission and value statements sound the same. Similarly, if you try to emulate someone else's values, you will inevitably fail to be motivated by them.

SELF-TEST: ESTABLISHING YOUR VALUES

Let's start with a fairly gentle questionnaire that may help you to get an initial sense of what you value in life. This is only a rough and ready quiz, and is designed to help steer you in the right direction. But you really do need to combine the results of this questionnaire with the other exercises in this chapter. After all, 20 questions cannot be enough to base the rest of your life on.

Read the following statements and tick as to whether you agree or disagree with each of the statements. Don't spend too much time thinking about any individual statement. Go through the statements fairly quickly and select the first answer that comes into your head.

Table 1.1

Question	Agree	Disagree
1. I would rather have power and status than help people		
2. I would quit my job if I thought it would make my family or partner happier		
3. I enjoy being assertive and influencing people		
4. Being able to provide financially for my family is more important than being there all the time for them		
5. Building good relationships at work is more important than focusing on the job itself		
6. I can usually get things done more effectively on my own without involving other people		
7. I genuinely enjoy being able to coach, train or develop colleagues		
8. I would rather be happy at home than successful at work		
9. I prefer to lead a team rather than work as an equal member of the team		
10. I enjoy being put under pressure to meet deadlines and attain challenging goals		
11. I would rather other colleagues took on the tedious tasks than volunteer to do them myself		
12. I tend to compare my pay and achievements with those of my friends and colleagues		

Scoring your self-test

In very broad terms, there are four main categories of values. Some people are motivated by the lure of having power and influence over others. Some people value their personal relationships, such as those with their partners, children, friends or families. Another group of people feel most motivated when they are able to help others. And the final group of people includes those who enjoy success for its own sake: being given credit and rewards for their efforts.

Look at the scoring table below and use it to calculate your scores for each of these four motivating forces. Which one is your primary motivating force? Write the four motivating forces down in a list from most important at the top down to least important at the bottom.

Table 1.2

	Influence	Personal	Helping	Achievement
Q1	Plus 2 if you agreed		Plus 2 if you disagreed	
Q2		Plus 2 if you agreed		*Minus* 2 if you agreed
Q3	Plus 2 if you agreed			
Q4		Plus 2 if you disagreed		Plus 2 if you agreed
Q5			Plus 2 if you agreed	
Q6	*Minus* 2 if you disagreed			Plus 2 if you agreed
Q7			Plus 2 if you agreed	
Q8		Plus 2 if you agreed		Plus 2 if you disagreed
Q9	Plus 2 if you agreed		Plus 2 if you disagreed	
Q10				Plus 2 if you agreed
Q11	Plus 2 if you agreed		Plus 2 if you disagreed	
Q12				Plus 2 if you agreed
Total score for each column =				

Understanding your scores

Look at the total scores under each column. Your highest score indicates your main motivating force – what you value above all else. The second highest score indicates your secondary motivating force – your second most important value. And so on.

Here are some brief thoughts about each of the four categories:

- **Influence.** People who score highly on this motivating force tend to enjoy having status and control. They like to be the leader in situations, and they enjoy being able to influence and cajole others. These people enjoy being managers.

- **Personal relationships.** This category describes people who most value their relationships outside of work. These people focus on their friends, family and other loved ones, and their world tends to focus very strongly on making their partner and/or family and friends happy. For these people, work is merely a means to an end: that of being happy at home.

- **Helping.** These people are most satisfied when they are helping others, perhaps by subtle encouragement and emotional support or more directly through coaching and training. They are most concerned with creating and sustaining relationships with the people – whether it is colleagues, customers, suppliers, or clients – that they work with.

- **Achievement.** These people enjoy success and most fear failure. They are not bothered about whether they work in a team or not, as long as they are able to get things done. They like to set challenging goals for themselves and enjoy being recognized and rewarded when they meet or exceed these goals.

Looking at your ordered list of the four motivating forces, how do you feel about your scores? Do you agree with the order of the list? Or do you think that the order is wrong, and if so, how would you re-write your list?

Remember that this is a quick self-test questionnaire to give you an idea of what your values may be, it is not meant to be a conclusive test. Whatever the results, though, it should have given you some ideas as to what you may value in your life. Now move on to the first exercise, which will help you to flesh out your values.

EULOGY EXERCISE

This exercise probably requires more thought and effort on your part than any other in this book. But if you give it your full attention, you may be surprised by what you can get out of it.

This exercise asks you to imagine a point in the distant future when you have died. If a close friend or colleague were writing a eulogy about your entire life, what would you like them to say about you? It is a cliché that no one on his or her deathbed ever said, 'I wish I'd worked harder.' So use this exercise as an opportunity to ask yourself 'What if…?'

The steps to doing this exercise are as follows:

1. Make sure that you have at least half an hour free to allow yourself to think without distraction.

2. Take a clean sheet of paper and write at the top of the page: 'My eulogy: how I would like to be remembered.'

3. Then write a detailed description of how you would like a close friend to describe you at your own funeral. You could write in prose or just a series of bullet points. This is not an essay that you ever need to show anyone else, you are using this exercise to try to discover what you might like to achieve with the rest of your life.

4. Think about both your professional and personal life. Think about all of the social relationships that you have: with friends, family, your local community, and so on.

5. Keep in mind that this is how you would *like* to be remembered: your eulogy should not be mired in mundane reality. Avoid taking your life and merely extrapolating more of the same until its end. The point is that by trying to think about how you would ideally like your life to turn out, you may uncover goals and aspirations that have been unrealized.

If you would prefer to do so, you could pretend that you were writing an obituary for a newspaper. What you write about will probably be very similar, but some people feel more comfortable with the writing style involved in composing an obituary.

Developing your eulogy further

When writing a eulogy, it can be easy to neglect or forget to cover certain areas of your working life. Here are some additional questions that may act as prompts and help you to flesh out your eulogy:

▓ What kind of financial reward do you need in your life?

▓ To what extent do you need status, promotions and job titles to make you feel good about yourself?

▓ How much do you need autonomy and independence in your work?

▓ How important is job security and regularity of income to you?

▓ How much do you like (or would you like) having responsibility for other people?

▓ To what extent do you seek out problems to solve and challenges to overcome in your work?

▓ What technical skills do you most enjoy using in your work?

▓ What personal, creative, spiritual or religious needs do you have?

▓ What kind of atmosphere or culture would you most like to have around you at work?

Critiquing your eulogy

Once you have finished the first draft of your eulogy, take a break. Go and do something else for a day or two, and then come back to it, add to it and make changes to it as new ideas come to you. If you feel comfortable doing so, discuss it with close friends or family members. Keep making changes to it until you are satisfied with it. Most people find that it takes at least a couple of hours of thinking time – perhaps spread over the course of a few weeks – to write a thorough eulogy that they are happy with.

Eventually, you will have a eulogy that you are fairly happy to progress with. Read through your eulogy and jot down some notes about the following questions:

How did you feel while you wrote your eulogy? What thoughts came to mind? Perhaps you thought, 'I'm wasting my time in my current job' or 'I need to reclaim my evenings and weekends from work.' Reading through your eulogy, does anything not quite ring true? Many people are tempted to include mention of social responsibility or spending more time with their family. But remember that this eulogy is for your eyes only. Many people find that their initial eulogies are written with a hidden observer looking over their shoulder and they write it as if their spouse or partner, or perhaps a parent or their circle of friends is judging them. But remember that this is about what will give you satisfaction in your career and happiness in your life. If you cannot be honest with yourself, what is the point in doing the exercise? So, if those things are not important to you do not include them, take them off the list.

What is the ARC of your life? ARC is an acronym for achievements, relationships, and characteristics. Draw up a table as below and fill it out accordingly, thinking about further questions as follows:

▮ What achievements does your eulogy talk about? Make a list of what you might like to accomplish with the rest of your life.

- What relationships does your eulogy mention? How do you aim to please the people that are close to you?
- What characteristics, qualities or traits does the eulogy mention about you? In particular, look for adjectives, adverbs and phrases that describe you and the way you do things.

Table 1.3

Achievements	Relationships	Characteristics

- What does the ARC table tell you about your personal goals? Do you feel that the list of achievements, relationships, and characteristics describes a future that you could see yourself fulfilling? And what does it tell you about the direction that you need to take from now on?
- Finally, does your eulogy excite or at least intrigue and interest you? If your eulogy is merely more of the same, in other words a straight continuation of what you are doing now, you might want to think about starting the exercise from scratch.

Once you are satisfied with your analysis of your eulogy, keep it in a safe place. And then give yourself a mental pat on the back: you have just completed a major exercise in setting a career direction for yourself.

Sample summary obituary:
James Cramer, current age: 45

James Cramer passed away yesterday afternoon at the age of 82. His son-in-law reported that he experienced chest pains while playing tennis. He is survived by a wife, two children and three grandchildren. He will be remembered for his leadership at New Advantage Pharmaceuticals. After taking on the role at the age of 43, he had set a goal to triple the size of the business within five years, something which he achieved within three years. He believed strongly that scale was necessary for the business, so he embarked on an ambitious campaign of acquisitions. He did not enjoy the tedium of running a stable business and lived for the challenge of broking deals and integrating new businesses.

James will also be remembered for his tireless work for a leukemia charity. At the age of 42, he saw his own son pass away with the disease, and a few years later he resolved to devote a significant proportion of his time working to raise funds for the charity.

He will be missed by his loved ones, many friends, and colleagues alike.

Sample summary eulogy:
Nathalie du Cadet, current age: 28

- Brought up three children who each flourished in their own ways, Nathalie was always proud of the fact that she did not push her children into a 'good profession' as her parents had done to her.
- Was recognized by friends and colleagues alike for having a strong sense of irony: in never taking herself, her work, colleagues or customers too seriously.
- Continued in the field of sales and marketing until her thirties, before deciding to complete an executive MBA to give her a wider, strategic perspective on sales and marketing. This quickly enabled her to move into general management roles where she was able to have complete profit and loss responsibility, which appealed heavily to her leadership streak.
- Enjoyed exercising her creative gifts. While her parents had encouraged her to take flute lessons in her early childhood, she had never enjoyed it. Under her own steam, she decided to take up lessons again, becoming an accomplished flautist and playing in a small wind band throughout her thirties and forties.
- Etcetera.

PRIORITIES EXERCISE

While writing your eulogy is an opportunity to think about long-term goals, it can sometimes be useful to think about the short-term priorities for this stage of your career. Your eulogy is something to aim for over the course of years, if not decades. But this exercise can help you to focus on the priorities that are important to you right now. These priorities may change over the coming months or few years: for example, equity ownership might not be an option where you work at the moment, but something that could be a priority when you come to do this exercise at a later date. Or perhaps you have children studying for exams who need a lot of time and attention for the next few years, but later when they have left home, you might have much more time to spend on yourself and your plans to travel the world. By doing this exercise periodically – perhaps every year or so – it will help you to further focus your efforts in improving and enriching your career.

The following is a randomly ordered list of 'motivators'. We can think of it as a more detailed analysis of the four motivating forces that we looked at in the previous exercise.

Table 1.4

The Motivators	
Challenging work	Contribution to society
Current income	Equity ownership
Family	Friends
Geographical location	Health
Influence at work	Job security
Leisure time	Loving partner
Personal growth	Personal possessions
Predictable working hours	Promotion
Spiritual growth	Supportive colleagues
Travel	Working environment
Your children	Wealth

Ranking

Your task is to take the list and put them in rank order of importance: placing the most important motivators at the top and the least at the bottom of the list. One way of doing this could be to write each item out on a fresh Post-It note, and to keep rearranging the list until you are satisfied with the ordering. Or alternatively, simply take a sheet of blank paper and rewrite the list.

I am often asked whether one is allowed to have tied rankings. Unfortunately, the answer is no. Life does not allow you the luxury of being indecisive. There are only 24 hours in the day. As the saying goes, 'You can't have your cake and eat it.' If you want to make your millions, you had better be prepared to give up those leisurely evenings and maybe even weekends. Or if you want to make a contribution to your community or society, is it compatible with your desire to be wealthy?

Understanding your priorities

Once your list is complete, you should think about what each of the motivating factors means to you personally. Scribble a few notes alongside of each word or phrase to define what it means to you in practical terms. For example, Nathalie's first three items might be:

1. Loving partner: 'To work hard at my relationship and never allow work to split us up as it did with my parents.'
2. Colleagues: 'To have supportive colleagues who I really enjoy working with. Having a good time for 8 hours a day is more important to me than earning a fortune.'
3. Your children: 'To have three children with David by the time I am 35.'

Finally, compare your list of rankings with how you spend your time in your life at the moment. If you say that you value certain priorities, then it should follow that you invest time and effort in them. Ask your partner or a close friend to give you an honest perspective about your list of priorities. Do they agree with your rankings? For example, if you say that you value your children above all else, would others agree that you consistently put them above your career and financial gain? Or if you say that you enjoy challenging work, do they see you as someone who constantly seeks out new job opportunities to keep from stagnating? As with the eulogy exercise, the danger here is that many people create a list of priorities that are more socially desirable to other people than real.

ENCAPSULATING YOUR VALUES

The eulogy exercise and priorities exercise should together help to give you a sense of some goals for your life. Now you should be ready to bring it all together. Americans often call this a 'life mission'. We do not need to be so grand. Why not simply call it your 'personal goal' or a 'career statement', if it makes you feel more comfortable to avoid any more management jargon!

Writing such a statement is worth doing because it will act as a quick reminder for what you have decided you want out of your life. Think about your long-term future. Do not be limited to only the next few years of your life. Try to project yourself at least five or ten years into the future.

Some example statements include:

■ 'I want to have a career that is fast-paced and challenging. I don't want to stagnate in a role that doesn't change at all. And I think that I will only get that sense of challenge by working in small, entrepreneurial businesses. I'm willing to put in the hours and the effort, but in return I expect to be rewarded well. And if those rewards are not forthcoming, I will always look to move on.'

■ 'I want to balance my working life against my family life. I need to feel valued by colleagues. I refuse to work in organizations where politicking or petty rivalries run amok. However, work is only a means to an end, so I want to have a life outside of my work that allows me to spend time with my wife and to see my children growing up.'

As you can see, these statements are not intended to lock you into a plan that will necessarily determine your every action for the next ten years. It is okay to have a *carpe diem* mindset: to take each day as it comes. But by having an idea of your values, you will be more easily able to meet the decisions and challenges of each day.

Testing your life mission

It is all very well to write a life mission statement for yourself that involves travelling the world with no belongings except for what you can carry in a backpack. However, is that really realistic? You may need to consider some of the constraints that may hold you back. Looking at the following factors, do you need to change your career goals at all?

▪ What **financial needs** do you or your family have? You might, for instance, want to re-train as a landscape gardener, but could you afford to take the pay cut?

▪ What **emotional needs** from your partner or any dependants do you need to factor into the equation? For example, do you want to spend certain times of day at home with your children?

▪ Are you in any way tied to a particular **geographical location**? And is it a genuine constraint limiting your career choices or just a nostalgic or emotional tie that you are reluctant to break?

▪ How is your **physical health**? Do you have any illnesses or physical conditions that you may need to take into account?

It is also worth checking market conditions against the career aspirations within your life mission. Again, it is easy to write a life mission for yourself about wanting to be a technology billionaire within the next decade, but is it possible? You may find it useful to talk through the work-oriented parts – as opposed to the personal parts – of your life mission to confirm that this is achievable for you.

Choose a few work acquaintances or industry sources that you believe are knowledgeable. Then talk through the following issues in relation to your life mission:

▪ What are the likely future developments in your industry? Thinking about the next five or ten years, how might market conditions change? Look at how globalization and technology, social and economic factors may affect your industry.

▪ How are these likely to affect your current employer? Is your current employer well or poorly placed to deal with these changes?

▪ What skills will be in greater demand in the future and what skills might be less important in the future? And what implications does this have for you and your future?

▪ How could changes in the world affect your ability to achieve your life mission? Thinking realistically, do you need to change your life mission at all?

Having thought about your career direction, the other chapters in this book will help you to achieve your career goals in life.

2

Beating office politics

The workplace is getting more competitive. As organizations downsize and de-layer, there are fewer opportunities for promotion. So it should come as no surprise that surveys repeatedly show that more and more people are complaining of being adversely affected by politicking.

Office politics can take many shapes and forms. At one end of the scale, there is outright manipulation, manoeuvring and backstabbing. But most of the time, politicking is far subtler: it comes in the guise of gossip with a slightly hurtful edge, or perhaps passing the blame on to someone else to save one's own neck. Even sly gossip or rumour mongering can be used to inflict damage on the reputations and careers of others.

One of the most important lessons you can learn is that **building relationships at work is as important as getting down to the tasks of whatever you do**. Getting a report out or closing a big deal with a customer simply does not matter if your colleagues do not like you and do not want to work with you. We can all think of people who consistently under-perform but get away with it because they use political tactics and are well regarded by people higher up in the organization. On the other hand, if the bosses do not like you, they will find some way to get rid of you, no matter how good you are with clients or customers. Of course, it is not right or fair. It just is.

However, simply seeking to make friends with everyone will not get you to your goal. For example you could end up volunteering to take on far more work than you can possibly do in an effort to please everyone. So that is not an answer either.

Politics is a part of organizational life. There will always be people who want to get ahead desperately enough to use such tactics without compunction. Whether you work with just 10 colleagues or 10,000, political activity is likely to be going on around you. If you want to survive, you will need to look out for yourself and learn how to disarm the office politicians.

SELF-TEST: IDENTIFYING POLITICS WHERE YOU WORK

Political activity goes on in most organizations, but it is worse in some than others. The first step in arming yourself against political attacks is to look at the extent to which politicking goes on where you work. Look at the following statements and tick either 'yes' or 'no' depending on whether you think it describes your workplace. To get an accurate score, you must answer every question.

Table 2.1

	Yes	No
1. Colleagues rarely own up for mistakes that they have made		
2. Official news often leaks out on the grapevine		
3. People talk about other colleagues behind their backs		
4. Good people rarely get overlooked for promotion		
5. People always share credit where it is due		
6. A lot of discussion goes on behind closed doors		
7. A few of my colleagues make cruel jokes about other people		
8. There are almost no cliques at work		
9. It is very difficult to keep anything quiet at work		
10. The best people usually rise to the top of this organization		

Scoring politics where you work

Calculate your organization's score as follows:

Award your organization a point for every 'yes' that you ticked: but only for questions 1–4, 6–7, and 9.

Add another point for every 'no' that you ticked for questions 5, 8 and 10.

Table 2.2

Your organization's score	Comment
1–3	Count yourself lucky, as you seem to be in a lucky minority of people. It seems that little politicking goes on where you work. On the other hand, are you simply being naïve? Try asking a trusted colleague whether he or she agrees with your analysis of whether politics happen around you or not.
4–6	Your workplace seems average in terms of its level of political activity. But average does not necessarily mean that you should accept it passively. You may sometimes feel that you get less recognition and respect than you deserve. You may occasionally feel left out or looked over. Or perhaps you have a lingering sense that you do not assert your rights as much as you should. The suggestions in this chapter may help you to make your working life easier for yourself.
7+	Your workplace is more political than most. The advice in this chapter will go some way towards dealing with immediate problems. But after taking this chapter into consideration, what you really need to do is look at Chapter 3 to understand how to take preventive action. As the adage goes, prevention really is better than cure.

RECOGNIZING POLITICAL PROBLEMS AT WORK

Office politicians are often intelligent people who, because they are not restricted like most of us by our consciences, are able to employ all manner of devious and underhand methods intentionally to get ahead at work. However, there is also a category of simply incompetent colleagues who may be causing you difficulties by completely unintentionally using these tactics too.

Political problems can take many shapes and forms. Some of these include:

▮ Distorting the facts (typically behind your back) or even telling outright lies to make you look bad.

▨ Fault-finding or persistent criticism of you, often done in public for maximum effect.

▨ Gossiping or spreading rumours behind your back.

▨ 'Forgetting' to include you in communications, meetings, training, social events or other activities.

▨ Taking responsibility away from you, perhaps under the guise of 'wanting to lighten your workload'.

SELF-TEST: MEASURING YOUR POLITICAL SKILL

Before we go on to talk about some of the ways in which you can defend yourself against political attacks, here is another questionnaire that may help you to analyse your current skill level when it comes to dealing with political troubles at work.

Simply tick whether you agree or disagree with each of the following statements.

Table 2.3

	Agree	Disagree
1. I get on with everyone in my department		
2. I ask for feedback from the people that I work with on my performance		
3. I don't like to be disturbed by other people when I work		
4. I volunteer for work committees and projects outside of the remit of my day-to-day job		
5. I try to avoid people who seem to have a problem with me		
6. I know many people outside my department		
7. I frequently go out with colleagues for lunch or social events		
8. Getting a task done on time is more important than people's feelings		
9. I don't like to interfere when I see colleagues doing poor quality work		
10. I have a mentor I can speak to outside my department		

Scoring your political skill

Add up your personal score as follows:

Give yourself one point for every 'agree' you ticked for questions 1, 2, 4, 6. 7, and 10, and give yourself another point for every 'disagree' you ticked for questions 3, 5, 8, and 9.

Table 2.4

Your score	Comment
1–3	Unfortunately, you seem to have almost no political awareness. Your natural preference seems to be to focus on your work and to avoid problematic people. If you allow this to continue, you could end up being very disappointed in your career: letting others overtake you on the career ladder, leaving you to have the least enjoyable and most poorly paid work.
4–6	You have a little political awareness, but not enough to watch your back for political knives. You may have a reasonable relationship with some of your colleagues at work. However, you are in danger of being marginalized by other colleagues. It is these other colleagues who may be tempted to take advantage of you, so look out.
7–9	You have a good deal of political awareness. You have a reasonable relationship with most of your colleagues. However, do not let yourself become complacent. Continue to seek feedback from others and continue to tackle problems that you may have with colleagues as quickly as you can. Nipping a problem in the bud may be a cliché, but it will make your life considerably easier.
10	You have an excellent relationship with your colleagues. You keep your ear close to the ground and tackle problems quickly and efficiently. If you continue with your present level of political sensitivity, you should find many opportunities opening up to you at work. However, be careful, there will always be people who may be jealous of your success.

SEEKING A SECOND OPINION

If you do find yourself with a problem, do not wait for it to go away. Depending on the reasons, it is unlikely to go away. Taking action will limit the pain for you and the damage to your reputation or career.

The following steps may help you:

1. **Identify the problem**. Avoid blundering into a confrontation with the individual that you feel is harming your reputation at work. Take some time away from the office to review the 'evidence' that you have collected in your mind. Spend some time thinking about options for dealing with the situation. Office politicians are usually too clever to engage in political warfare out in the open: most political activity is more subtle and underhand. Think about how foolish you could look if you blundered into a confrontation with a backstabbing colleague, armed only with half the facts and unrehearsed tactics for dealing with the problem.

2. **Take note**. If the attacks are openly malicious (for example, verbal or written abuse and threats), you may want to keep detailed notes with dates of instances of harassment or maltreatment. If you have any physical evidence – such as e-mails, memos, or even hand-scrawled notes – these could constitute an important part of your arguments. Events are often distorted by the passage of time, and details are critical if you want to confront the office politician. In a worst-case scenario, your notes could serve as valuable evidence at an industrial tribunal.

3. **Seek the reasons**. People can be negative, hostile, or under-mining for all sorts of reasons. As previously mentioned, your 'assailant' may be intentionally using such tactics to undermine you. Perhaps they are out to 'get you' for either a real or imagined grievance. Alternatively, your assailant may actually have no insight into the effects that their actions are

having on you. So try to understand why an individual is behaving in a particular way towards you, so that you can formulate an appropriate strategy for dealing with it.

4. **Take advice**. It is easy to feel hurt when you are on the receiving end of political tactics. You may find yourself acting defensively and irrationally. So it is worth taking the time to talk to someone outside of your team that you can trust. For example, do you know a colleague in a distant department? Or do you perhaps have an ex-colleague who has now left your current organization but who understands some of the personalities involved? Alternatively, an external mentor or coach can also act as a sounding board. Such people will give you an independent perspective and may be able to help you shed light on the problem and advise you on the most sensible course of action. For example, should you confront the difficult individual in person, or should you go straight to your manager, or would an approach to your HR department actually be the best course to take?

5. **Resist using the same tactics**. Remember that your assailant's political behaviour may not be intentional. So focus on dealing with the issues openly and constructively. Spreading rumours about the individual or using other such Machiavellian methods will only harm your own reputation with your colleagues in the long-term.

Talking to your assailant

If you and your external mentor or trusted colleague together decide that the problem can be handled without involving other people, you may decide simply to take a stand and confront your tormentor.

Set up an appointment to see the individual. Either find a meeting room where you will not be disturbed, or perhaps even leave the work environment to seek out a café where you can talk away from prying eyes. Rehearse what you are going to say then, calmly and rationally, put forward your point of view. Make sure that you approach such a discussion assertively, never aggressively. Try to stick to the facts and their impact on you, rather than making accusations. Explain that this is your perspective, and not necessarily the absolute reality of what may have been happening. Also, talk in the first person rather than talking about what the other person may be doing. For example, say: 'I get the feeling that I am being victimized' rather than 'You are victimizing me.'

Talk through your evidence, and then ask for reactions. You are likely to get one of three responses:

1. You might find that the individual is genuinely horrified by how you feel. He or she might not have realized that his/her behaviour was having such an effect on you, and might be genuinely surprised by how it was perceived. If this is the case, the individual might have been inadvertently using political tactics because he or she is either incompetent or lacking in self-awareness. Hopefully, the person will apologize and take immediate action to remedy the situation.

2. A deliberate and conniving individual might also feign surprise, horror or lack of awareness. He or she might then try to use charm to make you think that you are actually the one at fault. But do not fall for that ruse. If the person promises to change his or her behaviour, then monitor the situation closely to see if he or she does behave differently. If he/she does not, you may want to consider getting tougher (see below).

3. Many individuals will be angry and hostile at being confronted. This is a natural response. But if you focus on the facts and avoid becoming emotional or aggressive in return, the individual should eventually calm down. Then is the time to extract an apology and work together to come up with ways of improving the situation.

SELF-TEST: YOUR STYLE OF TACKLING TRICKY PEOPLE

The vast majority of office politicians can be handled by confronting them with the facts and asking them in a non-confrontational manner to change their behaviour. However, there are many ways to confront someone. The following questionnaire will give you an idea of your natural tendencies. Read through the list and fairly quickly tick whether you agree or disagree with the following statements. And be honest with yourself: otherwise there is no value in completing the questionnaire.

Table 2.5

	Agree	Disagree
1. I always give negative feedback in private		
2. I am less good at giving negative feedback than I am at praising and complimenting others		
3. I don't mind pointing out other people's faults by sending e-mails or writing memos		
4. I want to be liked by my colleagues as much as is practicable		
5. I try to give people small pieces of feedback as often as I can		
6. I feel that mistakes or inappropriate behaviour in others must always be tackled there and then		
7. I try to celebrate others' good work or achievements		
8. I give little praise and infrequently: it has to be earned		
9. I put off giving negative feedback for as long as possible		
10. I don't see the harm in pointing out other people's faults in public		
11. I sometimes let people off the hook because they may improve their own behaviour for the better anyway		
12. I think of specific examples to back up my arguments when giving feedback to other people		

Understanding your style

This questionnaire taps into three common approaches to dealing with difficult people. Add up your personal score as follows:

Table 2.6

	Avoiding scale	Aggressive scale	Assertive scale
Q1			Add 1 point if you ticked 'agree'
Q2	Add 1 point if you ticked 'agree'		
Q3		Add 1 point if you ticked 'agree'	
Q4	Add 1 point if you ticked 'agree'		
Q5			Add 1 point if you ticked 'agree'
Q6		Add 1 point if you ticked 'agree'	
Q7			Add 1 point if you ticked 'agree'
Q8		Add 1 point if you ticked 'agree'	
Q9	Add 1 point if you ticked 'agree'		
Q10		Add 1 point if you ticked 'agree'	
Q11	Add 1 point if you ticked 'agree'		
Q12			Add 1 point if you ticked 'agree'
Total score			

Which was your highest score? Each of the following scales is described as follows:

- **Avoiding**. You may be the sort of person who steers clear of dealing with people who are causing you difficulties. Perhaps you hope to minimize their effects on you by spending as little time around them as possible. Or perhaps you give only partial feedback that focuses on the plus points of others but not the areas that you are unsatisfied with. Unfortunately, this tactic will only make them stronger. Seeing you retreat will give them fresh confidence to take further liberties with you. You need to be more assertive in your approach.

- **Aggressive**. If you are not careful, you could easily fall into the category of people who are over-critical when tackling others. You might not give balanced praise: focusing on negative behaviour at the expense of compliments for deserved good work. Consequently, when you need to speak to people, there is a danger that they might simply switch off and be resistant to any messages that you have.

- **Assertive**. You balance positive and negative feedback equally: recognizing that negative feedback can only change other people's behaviour if you provide positive feedback to make them feel good and keep them on side. You avoid using inappropriate channels (such as memos or e-mail) for giving feedback and recognize that 'little and often' is the best way of changing the behaviour of others.

GETTING TOUGHER

When you encounter office politics, the most likely course of action is likely to be taking your assailant aside and talking to them. However, if your assailant refuses to respond and change their behaviour, you might need to take further action. If your manager is supportive, you should ask for his or her guidance on the matter. The next step might be to speak to someone in your human resources or personnel department in confidence, presenting your evidence to him or her. Together, you might decide to pursue action using the company's official grievance procedure, possibly involving not only the difficult person but also his or her manager.

If you work for a smaller business, you might not have the support of a full HR department. In such cases, you could seek external advice from:

- Your company's employee assistance programme (EAP). Ask to speak to a counsellor, explain the situation, and ask for their advice.

- Your local Citizen's Advice Bureau. Look them up in the phone book. They should be able to advise you on a course of action, such as whether it would be worth pursuing a claim against the individual in an employment tribunal.

- A local firm of solicitors. If you have some concrete evidence to back up your claims of harassment, you may be able to persuade a solicitor to take up your case on a 'no win, no fee' basis. However, be aware of the significant time, financial cost and effort involved in taking something to the High Court, not to mention the risk of losing.

3

Exerting influence at work

The people I coach often say they feel that they are not given the respect they deserve. However, it is often the case that they do not receive any respect because they do not influence and persuade others effectively.

Think about it: you could be your organization's expert on a particular topic but fail to be acknowledged for it, if you cannot communicate it well to colleagues and customers. Perhaps you have brilliant ideas, but what use are they if you cannot explain them and persuade people to accept them?

If you want to carve a career out for yourself, you need to learn these subtle skills. People are not always swayed by logic. For example, people will often go out of their way to repay a favour or to help out a friend, even if logic dictates that it is not necessarily the best course of action. In recent years, many of these skills have been collected under a new heading called 'emotional intelligence' or EQ. This chapter shows you how to use different emotionally intelligent influencing styles to get others to help you in your career.

SELF-TEST: IDENTIFYING YOUR STYLE OF INFLUENCING

The first step is to identify your current, typical style of influencing others. Without a greater self-awareness of how you typically behave, you will not be able to understand how you need to change your behaviour. Most of us tend to have strengths in some areas and weaknesses in others: only the most adept influencers are able to switch between styles without missing a beat. This questionnaire is quite comprehensive – it has 24 questions – but it should still only take just over five minutes to complete. Again, be honest with yourself. Read each of the statements and try to decide on a rating for yourself based on the following four-point scale:

Table 3.1

1	2	3	4
'Hardly ever'	'Occasionally'	'Usually'	'Almost always'

Table 3.2

	Your score

1. I enjoy using facts and figures to back up my arguments
2. I listen to other people's concerns before putting forwards my own ideas
3. I set clear expectations for what I require of other people
4. I try to modify my responses to take into account other people's concerns
5. I am quick to admit when I am wrong
6. I find it easy to criticize the suggestions of other people
7. I compliment other people's ideas in order to show my appreciation of them
8. I am not afraid to give ground to ensure that I get what I really need
9. I focus on the pros and cons of an argument
10. I aim to find 'win/win' situations that will make both myself and the other party happy
11. I try to establish clear objectives and deadlines for delivery of work
12. I enjoy negotiating
13. I quickly identify the costs and benefits associated with different courses of action
14. I enjoy playing devil's advocate with other people's ideas
15. I put myself into others' shoes to understand what motivates them
16. I reward people well for hard work and success
17. I make sure that everyone has a chance to contribute ideas to a discussion
18. I like applying logic to problems and new situations
19. I monitor the progress of a task or project to make sure that no one is getting behind
20. I strive to meet people's personal as well as professional needs
21. I believe that a little give and take is important
22. I feel that people are most motivated by definite deadlines
23. I try to energize colleagues with a vision of what we can achieve
24. I am not afraid to tackle under-performance

Calculating your preferred influencing style

Use the following table to add up the scores for each of the four influencing styles. This may take you a few minutes, but it is worth doing carefully to make sure that you correctly identify your natural preferences.

Table 3.3

Influencing style		Your score
Convincing	Add up the scores from questions 1, 6, 9, 13, 14, 18	
Cajoling	Add up the scores from questions 2, 7, 15, 17, 20, and 23	
Commanding	Add up the scores from questions 3, 11, 16, 19, 22, 24	
Compromising	Add up the scores from questions 4, 5, 8, 10, 12, 21	

Now look at your pattern of scores. If you have fairly evenly balanced scores – within two or three points of each other – then you are one of those rare individuals who can change influencing styles easily to fit the needs of different situations.

However, most people will tend to have much higher scores on one or two of the influencing styles than others. On which influencing style do you have the highest score? This is your natural preference for influencing others.

UNDERSTANDING DIFFERENT INFLUENCING STYLES

Each of the four influencing styles has its merits and demerits, depending upon the circumstances. None is better than any of the others. As a proactive worker, you should be able to switch between different styles to get what you want. The four influencing styles are described as follows.

Influencing style: convincing

People who use the convincing style tend to influence others through logic and reason. They think through the advantages and disadvantages of different courses of action. These people enjoy a good debate, but in the sense of presenting facts and figures and defending them rather than getting into a heated and emotional confrontation. People who use this style are often described as:

- rational;
- critical;
- analytical;
- cool-headed;
- thorough.

This is a good style particularly when you are trying to present an argument that has tangible goals and outcomes. For example, when there are options that have clearly identifiable costs or benefits attached to them. This style is also good when you are giving formal presentations, perhaps a sales pitch to a new customer or client. Or if you need to present a business case to a group of colleagues, you will need to have done your research to make sure that you have all of the right facts and that your calculations are correct. Also, this style of influencing typically presupposes that there is a right or wrong answer.

However, this style is not appropriate for all situations because people are not inherently rational. For example, we all know the benefits of exercising more, eating more healthily, and smoking and drinking less, but most people ignore the advice precisely because they are not rational. Or we recognize that we should spend less of our money and save more, but so few of us do! Consequently, using a convincing style all of the time will not get the best results. In fact, using a convincing style can be associated with certain downsides:

▥ You may not always take into account other people's feelings. For example, people would often rather carry on with what they are doing rather than be told that they are wrong and be made to feel stupid.

▥ In one-to-one situations, people are rarely persuaded by facts alone. At work, for example, people often prefer to take the course of action that is *easiest* rather than the one that is *best* for the company.

▥ Many people would rather listen to people who they *trust*, rather than people who are right.

Influencing style: cajoling

People who are good at cajoling are good at making others feel valued. They focus on the needs of other individuals rather than the needs of the task at hand. Cajolers are good listeners and they build rapport effectively, share their own experiences, and try to put themselves into the other person's shoes. As a result, they are often able to generate a feeling of enthusiasm in others. Rather than focusing on facts and figures, these people focus on creating a feeling of trust. People who influence through cajoling are often described as:

▥ reliable;

▥ charming;

▥ optimistic;

▥ supportive;

▥ empathetic;

▥ idealistic.

Trying to cajole others is particularly effective when the logic behind an argument is not sufficiently cut and dried for a clear course of action to emerge. This is also a great style to adopt when you are trying to pull a team together and get them committed to achieving a long-term goal. This is also a particularly useful skill in trying to build up a strong network of people around you, you may not want anything from them right now, but by getting to know them and making them like you, you may be able to request favours of them later on.

Again, however, cajoling does not work all of the time. It takes time to listen to others and to build a rapport and feeling of trust. So, for example, when you are meeting a group of people for the first time, you are unlikely to be able to spend enough time with each of them to understand what each person's needs are likely to be. Consequently, adopting a cajoling approach can be associated with certain risks:

▌ You can invest too much time trying to establish a rapport and make a joint decision when the matter may require someone to make a quick decision.

▌ Others may be tempted to take advantage of your good will. They may come to realize that you will try to meet their personal needs, and exploit you to get what they want: perhaps by promising to do something for you in the long term if you will only do something for them more immediately.

▌ You could get overlooked for jobs that require an assertive or dynamic form of leadership.

Influencing style: commanding

Commanding others is a very assertive style of influencing others. It involves taking the lead in a discussion and setting out clear guidelines or expectations as to what is required of others. People who use this style a lot tend to be quite driven to achieve. They believe that hard work and results should be rewarded, perhaps by deserved praise or by hard cash. On the other hand, they feel that people who do not put effort into their work or deliver results should be disciplined. Managers who use this style will tend to give unambiguous instructions and provide clear deadlines for when they expect work to be completed. People who rely on commanding others are often described as:

- authoritative;
- determined;
- forceful;
- confident;
- articulate;
- hard-headed.

Commanding others is particularly appropriate when time is of the essence. When there is a crisis and simply not enough time to sit around throwing ideas around, someone needs to take the lead by analysing the situation quickly and making decisions as to who needs to do what. You may want to get some input into a discussion, but once you have made up your mind, you expect others to do their part. People who are good at commanding also tend to be the best at dealing with underperformance, as the other three styles tend to let lazy or ineffective colleagues and malingerers off the hook.

As with each of the other styles, you could come unstuck if you use commanding all of the time. Typically, you can only command people when they work for you: this style is inappropriate for dealing with your own boss or your peers. Peers may let you get away with ordering them around once or twice, but never more than that. In addition, even employees who report to you do not enjoy being told what to do for every minute of the day and can end up fairly demoralized by working for what they see as a controlling manager. As such, this style has a number of downsides:

- Telling people what to do tends to rely on position or status, so it can create resistance. If people decide that they do not want to do what you tell them, they could decide to rebel or subvert your instructions.

▮ Continual use of this style of influencing may make people dislike you. They may avoid dealing with you, with the result that you may be excluded from communication and social activities.

▮ Other people may see you as someone who is good at getting things done, but not at creating good feelings with your colleagues.

Influencing style: compromising

Compromising is a very practical way of influencing others. People who compromise well tend to focus on reaching solutions rather than getting every single point on their wish lists. The focus is on finding an outcome that all parties can at least be partly satisfied with. Bargaining and negotiating skills are key to reaching a speedy and effective compromise. Rather than arguing a single point of view, these individuals are good at looking for trade-offs: yielding some of what they want to get what they need. In addition, such individuals are good at talking up what they have gained and minimizing what they had to give up. People who attempt to compromise a lot of the time may be described as:

▮ conciliatory;

▮ pragmatic;

▮ matter-of-fact;

▮ weak-willed;

▮ reasonable.

People who use the compromising style of influence tend to be good at resolving situations where the two sides may seem entrenched in their beliefs. For example, if you are arguing for more flexible working hours, you may be willing to concede some of the other benefits that you currently have. Or if two sides are locked in a head-to-head confrontation, you are the type of person who can be brought in to mediate the dispute.

However, an undue focus on compromising could make other people perceive you as lacking backbone. There may, for example, be situations where there is no room for compromise, such as when you are arguing with someone over whether they made a mistake or not. They either made the mistake or they did not: there is not always a middle ground. As such, the risks attached in trying to reach compromises all of the time include that:

▨ You may sometimes attempt to compromise even though the other person is actually in the wrong. You might actually have been better off being more assertive.

▨ You may sometimes give away too much, too soon.

▨ People could see you as a bit of a pushover when it comes to making decisions.

Looking back at your scores

There really are no right or wrong answers to this questionnaire, as each style of influencing is appropriate in different circumstances. For example, when you are asked to give a formal presentation, then convincing is likely to be the most suitable. When you are trying to negotiate more flexible working hours, the cajoling and compromising styles may be equally appropriate. On the other hand, when there is a fire in the building and smoke billowing into the office, cajoling is the last thing you should be doing: someone needs to take charge and command others into taking quick action to save lives.

Now look back at the statements that relate to the influencing style on which you got the lowest score. This is your weakest area, the style that you use the most infrequently. Go back to the questionnaire and identify the individual statements that relate to it. How could you work harder to use those behaviours more often?

EXERCISE: PUTTING INFLUENCING INTO ACTION

Given that none of the four influencing styles can be the best for all situations, you must think about the suitability of each of them. Given the circumstances and perhaps individuals that you are trying to influence, how can you tailor your approach to make them side with you?

This exercise asks you to think about recent and current situations in which you have tried to persuade others. If you take the time to think through all of the questions, this will begin to make you more aware of alternative styles of influencing. In turn, this will make you more effective at influence and persuasion.

For each scenario, you may want to jot a few notes on a pad. Avoid just skimming through the questions very quickly. The real value of this exercise comes in thinking carefully about each of the questions, coming up with your own answers, and understanding its implications for how you could change your preferred style of influencing others.

Scenario one

1. First, think about your current organization. Who is the most difficult person that you currently work with?

2. What exactly do you find difficult about them? What do they say that annoys you? Thinking about the four styles, what do you think is their style of influencing?

3. How would you like that person to behave differently? Try to think of measurable objectives. So, rather than saying that you would like someone to be 'a better team player', it is more useful to think about what that would look like in practice: for example 'turning up to more team meetings, making more contributions during meetings, and taking on an equal share of the workload'.

4. When you have clashed or had difficulties with this person in the past, what influencing style did you use?

5. Finally, if you want to achieve the behaviour changes that you identified in question 3, which influencing style should you try to use in the future? How will you broach the subject and what will you say exactly?

Scenario two

1. Think about what you most want in your current job. What exactly is it that you want?

2. Who is (or who are) the person(s) who have the ability to give you what you want?

3. Looking back at the influencing style questionnaire, which was your preferred style of influencing, and how appropriate do you think that style would be for getting what you want?

4. Looking at the three other styles of influencing, what could be an alternative method of influencing? For example, could you cajole them by building a long-term rapport with those people to make them like and value you and want to give you what you want? Or could you convince them by demonstrating through some form of analysis the merits of your case? Or would identifying potential concessions be a valid route?

5. Having considered all four styles, which one will you choose?

6. And over what period of time will you try to achieve what you want?

Scenario three

1. This final scenario is about failure. When was the last time you failed to get something that you wanted from someone?

2. Try to recall the details. What did you want, what did you say or do? And what response did you get from the other person or people?

3. Looking back at that event, which influencing style do you think you adopted?

4. Finally, in retrospect, could you have tried one of the other influencing styles?

FINAL THOUGHTS

Your influencing style is not immutable. The whole purpose of completing the questionnaire and going through the different scenarios above is to help you modify your style to fit different situations.

People do change over time, especially when they move to new jobs, confront new cultures and take on new responsibilities. Why not complete the influencing styles questionnaire again in, for example, a year's time to see whether you have managed to take a more balanced approach to influencing and persuading others?

4

Investing in your CV

Gone are the days when employees were expected to get on with their jobs, hoping that their bosses would notice them and reward them for hard work and good results. Nowadays, you could work tirelessly for your employer, only to be made redundant by a cost-cutting drive from the overseas parent company or a downsizing exercise due to a downturn in the economy. If your organization needs to make people redundant, no one can guarantee that you might not be one of the casualties.

In such times, you need to be able to fend for yourself. The threat of losing your job is one of the strongest ties that bind you to your employer. By increasing your employability, you can take control of your career. The benefits of investing in your CV include:

- Better promotion prospects within your company, as colleagues recognize the key skills that you have.
- A reduction in the risk that you will be made redundant when jobs are being cut around you. Some commentators

refer to this as 'recession proofing' as organizations naturally want to get rid of the 'dead wood' first.

▓ Enhanced job opportunities outside of your current employer. If you invest in your CV, you may find that there are better offers elsewhere.

▓ A greater freedom to take some chances in your career: should you want to. In the bad old days of 'a job for life', employees used to think of the decision to desert a secure employer for a new one as risky. However, if you are confident in the skills and experience on your CV, you can take chances in the knowledge that you will always be able to find another job should things not turn out as you had expected.

▓ A quicker and smoother transition to a new job, should you wish to switch companies. People who have more skills and experiences on their CVs tend to get invited to more interviews.

You might be reading this and thinking that you eventually would like to be running your own business and that it therefore will not matter what you have on your CV as you will be your own boss. However, employers look for these skills because *these are the skills that make organizations successful.* Whether you are working for someone else or working for yourself: these are the skills that will help you to impress future customers or clients.

So what are the skills and experiences that will not only look good on your CV but also stand you in good stead for chasing the sorts of jobs and career fulfilment that you want?

SELF-TEST: MEASURING YOUR CORE COMPETENCIES

Before we move on to the key skills that you need to really get yourself noticed at work, let us look at the more basic skills that you should have. The term 'competency' is simply a word that a lot of businesses have adopted to describe the skills and behaviours that are linked to success at work. Before we can think about your ability to make change happen, for instance, we should think about whether you have good planning and communication skills. To use an analogy, you cannot run before you have learnt to walk.

The following questions ask you to rate your own skills against a set of skills. Think about each one in turn, but try to appraise yourself as honestly as possible. Use the following rating scale:

Table 4.1

1	2	3	4	5
'Worse than most people I know'	'Needs some work'	'Equally as good as my peers'	'Better than some of my peers'	'Better than most people I know

If you feel that a statement does not apply to you at all, then give yourself a zero score for that question.

Table 4.2

	Your score
1. Consistently hitting deadlines	
2. Writing concise and clear e-mails, memos and reports	
3. Volunteering to take part in committees and teams	
4. Getting other people involved in discussion before making a decision	
5. Reading a broadsheet newspaper frequently	
6. Demonstrating visible enthusiasm for my work	
7. Being driven to achieve at work	
8. Understanding what people in other departments do	
9. Taking on tasks that other colleagues do not want to do	
10. Quickly gathering facts and figures to analyse the pros and cons of a situation	
11. Giving presentations that retain other people's attention	
12. Following market trends in my industry	
13. Planning my time in advance to focus on the priorities for each day	
14. Understanding the strategy of my company and how it affects my day-to-day job	
15. Articulating my arguments clearly	
16. Sharing credit with other members of a team	
17. Weighing up other options before choosing a particular course of action	
18. Being aware of what competitors to my company are doing	
19. Speaking confidently in meetings and other group settings	
20. Managing conflict and seeking consensus within team meetings	
21. Getting at the root cause of a problem rather than tackling the symptoms	
22. Getting tasks done that others have given up on	
23. Explaining technical matters to people who are not technical experts	
24. Ensuring that quieter members of the team have a chance to make a contribution	
25. Making tough decisions in uncertain circumstances	

Scoring the competency questionnaire

Use the following table to add up the scores for each of the six work competencies. There are quite a few numbers to add up, so take your time.

Table 4.3

Work skill		Your score
Communication	Add up the scores from questions 2, 11, 15, 19 and 23	
Reasoning	Add up the scores from questions 4, 10, 17, 21 and 25	
Teamwork	Add up the scores from questions 3, 9, 16, 20 and 24	
Business awareness	Add up the scores from questions 5, 8, 12, 14 and 18	
Achievement-orientation	Add up the scores from questions 1, 6, 7, 13 and 22	

What were your highest scores in, and what were your lowest scores in? Look at the descriptions below, and focus on your two lowest scores. Or, if you had more than two competencies where you scored less than 15 points, you should think about putting some effort into improving all of those areas. If you are serious about boosting your CV, it will take effort.

Understanding the core competencies

These core competencies are merely the generic skills that almost all employers look for in their workforce. Whether you are a director, a manager, a shop floor worker or an administrator, the people in charge will expect you to either have these skills, or at least have the potential to develop them very quickly.

Read through the description of each competency. Then try to think about how you might work on the scores that you did not score so highly on. What training courses or self-development programmes could you go on? Are there colleagues that you could trust to mentor you and give you feedback and guidance in those competencies? Or what about projects that you could get involved in to give you more experience in using those competencies?

Communication

People with good communication skills can make themselves clearly understood in a variety of ways. Communication could take the form of a hastily typed e-mail or a carefully composed letter, a one-to-one discussion with a colleague, or a formal presentation to a group of potential customers. It hardly needs explanation why communication skills are paramount to being employable.

In terms of improving your CV, you should think about writing down examples of presentations that you have given, as well as reports or papers that you have written.

To boost your communication skills, you could try to:

■ Identify role models amongst your colleagues who you think are good communicators. Then observe them and try to learn from what they say or do. Is it something about their body language that makes them effective communicators, or perhaps the words that they choose? Once you have observed them for a while, are there any of those words or behaviours that you could adapt and adopt yourself?

■ Spend more time preparing before you have to speak in meetings. For example, if you need to give a presentation, you should definitely think about preparing the presentation a few days beforehand and taking it somewhere quiet – like your home – and rehearsing out loud.

■ Show important written work to a colleague that you can trust. Ask him or her to proofread it and see whether it makes sense. If not, ask for suggestions as to how you could make it punchier.

Reasoning

People with highly developed reasoning skills are good at gathering information – whether it is facts, figures, or even other people's opinions – and then choosing a course of action. This does not necessarily mean that someone who is good at reasoning must always spend a very long time gathering data, as there is often not enough time to ponder over different options for too long. Quick decisions sometimes need to be made or the opportunity could just go away. However, when quick decisions do need to be taken, the individual with good reasoning skills will observe the results of that decision – right or wrong – and seek to learn from it.

Organizations are constantly looking out for people who can reason well and make good judgements. Organizations do not like ditherers who cannot make up their minds; neither do they like people who jump to conclusions without gathering all of the facts. In terms of your CV, you should work up to being able to write down a few examples of key decisions that you had a part in making.

If you found that reasoning was not one of your strengths, then you could think about making efforts to:

- ▮ Seek alternative options whenever you have the time to think about a decision. Rather than presenting a single course of action to others, you should always think about a range of options. It is harder for other people to object when you have different options.

- ▮ Try to consult as widely as you can to ensure that you have all of the facts and perspectives that you need to make a decision. Remember that few decisions can be based on entirely concrete facts. Most decisions need to take into account other people's feelings and opinions too.

▮ Take the occasional risk. If your natural tendency is not to make decisions, then you should just take more chances. Of course, no one is asking you to put safety or vast sums of money at risk. But sometimes taking almost any course of action is better than doing nothing. However, when you have made the decision, always monitor how the situation turns out and try to learn from your mistakes.

Teamwork

You are probably sick of hearing from colleagues about the importance of teamwork. However, this is one of the absolutely key skills that organizations look for. No matter how good you are at the technical aspects of your job, you are no good to anyone unless you can deal with other people and share your ideas and work with each other. Good team players are able to contribute to team discussions but at the same time encourage others to participate in the discussion, perhaps by acknowledging the contribution that others make. People with highly developed team skills will also be able to recognize the relative strengths and weaknesses of individual team members and suggest breaking up work tasks to suit those strengths and weaknesses.

If the questionnaire identified that you have a low team score:

▮ Try to volunteer or sign up for a team such as a committee, working group, or project team. The team need not be in the workplace, it could just as easily be a community group or perhaps a committee for a local charity, club or society. There may not be one that you can join straight away, so keep on the look out for one. The team does not have to be particularly large or meet that often, but it will help you to get used to contributing in a group setting. Even if you feel uncomfortable with the thought of pitching yourself into a team environment, this is the only way you will improve your team skills. You may at first resent the extra work that this may mean for you, but it will encourage you to build up your team skills very quickly.

■ In team meetings, look out for the group dynamic. Who looks shy, quiet, or uncomfortable speaking up? Who is loud and vociferous? Then think about how you can help the quieter people to speak up more and prevent the louder members of the team from dominating the discussion.

■ When you have completed one team project look out for a second one. Perhaps when you have completed that one, look out for a third, larger team project, and so on. Each team project that you get involved in should add further weight to your CV.

Business awareness

Getting on with the day-to-day tasks in your job is all very well, but organizations are increasingly looking for people who can take a more strategic view of their work: for example, keeping up-to-date with the latest developments in your field. But having a good level of business awareness also involves having an understanding of what customers want as well as trends in the marketplace. An appreciation of what the competition is getting up to will also impress bosses and future employers.

In surveys, employers also frequently complain that employees do not have enough understanding of what goes on outside of their particular fields of expertise. Sales people, for example, do not tend to know enough about HR issues, while marketing people may not have a good enough understanding about the finance function.

Developing greater business awareness can be achieved if you:

■ Read more to do with your specialist area. So take up a subscription to your trade publication, especially as this can often be claimed back as a professional membership on your annual tax return.

▨ Read more *outside* of your area of specialism. The 'quality' newspapers will help to expand your level of knowledge. *The Financial Times*, in particular, is packed with a variety of articles that will broaden your knowledge and give you at least a passing familiarity with the new concepts and ideas in the world of work. If you work in the public sector, then try to learn more about the private sector, and vice versa.

▨ Keep mobile in your career. Rather than risk stagnating in your job, you must keep looking for new projects. So, if you are going to stay with the same company for more than three or four years, would it be possible to move into a different department or a new role? If you are going to have the same role and job title for more than two or three years, what new projects can you embark on to demonstrate that you have not allowed yourself to get complacent? Or perhaps it may be time to look outside of your present employer for a new name to add to your CV?

Achievement orientation

This competency is to do with the extent to which you put effort into achieving results. Someone with a high score will tend to be self-motivated and able to persevere even when others give up. An achievement-oriented individual will invest energy into hitting deadlines and meeting goals – preferring to make small personal sacrifices such as staying late at work or getting to work early – rather than let other people down.

Furthermore, such an individual will tend to set high personal standards and also expect other people to perform to these high standards. As a result, someone with a high achievement orientation is recognized by colleagues and bosses alike as someone who can be relied upon to get a job done, the kind of person who works hard and who deserves to be rewarded well.

This competency is not so much of a skill as a mindset. To become more achievement oriented, you need to:

- Set yourself short-term goals and reward yourself for reaching them. Setting measurable and realistic goals is a well-known way to improve motivation in short bursts. For example, you might promise to buy yourself something or otherwise treat yourself if you complete a project successfully.

- Ask your HR department if you can go on a time management course. Such courses can often give you practical tips for getting unpleasant, but necessary tasks done more quickly, enabling you to free up more of your day to do the work that you enjoy more. If you do not have access to such courses at work, you could try looking on the Internet or trying www.learndirect.co.uk which is a government-sponsored training Web site.

- Identify what would motivate you more. Look back at your eulogy and the various other exercises from Chapter 1. It is very difficult to force yourself to be passionate about work without something that truly motivates you. So if your current role, colleagues or company do not fill you with much enthusiasm you may need to think about moving on.

EXERCISE: STOP, START AND CONTINUE

The previous section on core competencies should have helped you to understand the skills that you need to foster and develop in order to further your career aims. However, there is a clear difference between mere understanding and doing. Understanding that we should do something is very different from knowing that we will do it.

However, psychologists have identified that people who take the time to think through a plan of action are much more likely to succeed in changing their behaviour. The following three boxes provide you with space to jot down ideas for what you could do differently either immediately or in the very near future. Simply take a pencil and write down a few thoughts in each box, or copy each table out onto three separate sheets of A4.

Table 4.4

I will stop ...

Table 4.5

I will start ...

Table 4.6

I will continue ...

FURTHER SKILLS

Now that we have covered the essential skills, let us look at some of the more advanced skills that will set you apart from the rest of the organization. Research shows that certain skills are particularly well regarded by employers. These are:

▦ working across teams;

▦ managing change;

▦ delivering organizational benefits;

▦ continuing professional and personal development.

Working across teams

We have already talked about the core competency of teamwork. However, the 21st century organization is not just looking for the person who can work within a team, but also the kind of person who can work across teams. Companies that have exhausted their traditional markets are being forced to explore new territories for customers, typically in Eastern Europe, the Far East and South America.

This means that organizations are increasingly looking for people who can work across boundaries in this global environment. In practice, this means being able to work with other teams perhaps across departments, divisions or even countries. The term 'silo mentality' is often used to describe people who are unable to work effectively with other parts of the organization. Two common examples of employees with a silo mentality include:

▦ People who have worked in head office roles for most of their career without getting some field or operational experience.

▦ People who have worked within only one function, field or area of expertise and have not broadened their outlook by working in a different function.

If any of those describe you at all, you may need to consider a move of some sort. Being able to work in multicultural teams, build relationships, and negotiate with managers, customers, and suppliers from different cultures is becoming increasingly important. Moreover, as the vast majority of the working population are unwilling to make the move abroad, the demand for such people typically outstrips the supply, with the result that the people who are willing and able to do it can often be rewarded very well.

If you work for a large, multinational employer, then international opportunities may be fairly easy to find. Many such companies have secondment programmes where they will send employees with a good track record overseas. Typically it is a lateral move rather than a promotion, but the understanding will usually be that you will be promoted, or given much greater responsibility, on your return to your home country.

However, if you work for a much smaller organization, then secondment may not be an option. So you may need to think about looking for a new employer, and keep an eye out specifically for the opportunities for an international transfer with that new organization. You could even think about a change of career for a few years, as jobs such as management consultancy, sales and business development can often require you to work for brief spells of weeks or months in other countries.

Before you rush to apply for that posting in Kazakhstan, though, you may want to think through the following questions:

▪ How will you surmount the language barrier? In many subsidiaries of UK or American companies, the business language may be English, but the socializing and gossip around the coffee machine will typically be in the local language. Will your employer provide lessons for you or will you need to pay for a short course of tuition yourself? Obviously, having a grasp of the local language will be of much greater value to your CV.

▓ How will the move affect your personal circumstances? If you have a family, spouse or partner, how willing would they be to move with you, and how easily would they be able to find work? Typically, countries outside the European Union have quite tough policies, making it difficult for foreigners to get jobs, their concern being that foreigners will swamp the local job market, raising local unemployment.

▓ What bureaucratic hoops will you need to jump through? Often, to get a work permit or visa, you need to demonstrate that you are bringing specialist skills that cannot be provided by a local citizen.

▓ What will your job role actually involve on a day-to-day basis? For example, if you are merely building spreadsheet models in a back office, it makes almost no difference what part of the world you are in. How much contact will you have with colleagues, as well as local suppliers and customers? Again, the more interaction you have with the local marketplace, the more 'saleable' you will be back in your home country.

▓ Finally, who will mentor or sponsor you while you are away? Do not be surprised if you find yourself committing at least a few cultural gaffes, and when that does happen, who will you turn to for ideas and support to deal with any problems?

If you are determined enough, though, working across teams – and especially working across international teams – will boost both your pay and your future prospects.

Managing change

'Change management' is another big buzz phrase in our increasingly competitive world. Customers are increasingly demanding new products and better service, but at a lower cost. So change is becoming a requirement in organizations, from the very large multinational right through to the small business that might employ three people in someone's spare room. Even the small business is not immune to change, and has to think about everything from new IT systems and new software to changes in legislation about data protection and the provision of pensions.

As organizations struggle to change their ways of working, they need individuals who can help them to revamp what they do and make change happen. Getting involved in change demonstrates not only to your current employer but also to future employers that you are a forward-looking individual. And given that most employees see change as a nuisance, the few who enjoy making change happen are in short supply.

Change projects come in a variety of guises. They may be called cost reduction programmes, relocation schemes, process improvement teams, post-merger integration teams, total quality programmes, and so on. All of these can be opportunities for you to make your CV stand out from the crowd.

Large-scale change

Change often arrives as a sweeping organization-wide initiative. Such large-scale change often involves external management consultants and a lot of communication from senior managers about the new direction of the business. Large-scale change is often triggered by external events such as a merger or acquisition, a plunge in the share price, or a dramatic change in customer demands.

When such announcements are made, you should seize your opportunity to ask around to see if you can be invited onto a change team. Typically, teams will be put together to look at particular issues. For example, there may be a team looking at a new IT system or database. Another team might look at new contracts and HR processes. Perhaps another team will look at changing marketing and other promotional material. There is usually plenty of work to go around, so your invitation to take part will almost certainly be accepted with gratitude.

Small-scale change

However, not all change is so sweeping. Change happens all of the time on a daily basis at a team or departmental level, and the way to get involved in making these sorts of change happen is to watch what is going on around you. What are the problems that continually crop up in your department? What are people constantly frustrated about? Even if they are relatively minor, there could be an opportunity for you to think about making the problem go away. If you have even a vague idea of how those problems could be tackled, you could discuss your ideas with your boss. Suggest that you and a few colleagues brainstorm ideas and put together a business case about the costs and benefits of making those problems go away. However, be aware that the biggest obstacles to change are rarely the financial or technical problems that may come with it, but the resistance from fellow employees who may dislike having to do things differently. It will take all of the influencing skills of a master office politician (see Chapter 3) to persuade your colleagues to take the changes on board.

Most people who get involved in change projects find it hugely satisfying. They report feeling that they are making a difference while at the same time adding valuable experience to their CV. And remember: all of the time that you are tackling problems at work, you are simultaneously creating a reputation amongst colleagues as a change manager as well as bulking up your CV.

Delivering organizational benefits

Being hard-working is not necessarily a good thing. Think about it. If someone slaves away all day but achieves very little, then *from an employer's perspective* that employee is not much better than someone who is lazy and achieves little.

Employers value employees who can deliver outcomes that demonstrably help the organization to achieve its aims. You may hear some employers talk about wanting employees who can 'add value' to their organization. Such 'value adding' outcomes include:

- increased profit or market share;
- reduction in cost;
- greater speed, efficiency or time savings;
- increased product quality;
- better relationships with customers, clients, suppliers, or other stakeholders;
- improved morale of colleagues.

This has two main implications for people wanting to invest in their CVs. First, look at your actual curriculum vitae, the one that you last used or are using to apply for jobs. Make sure that your CV to date shows identifiable achievements. Prospective employers do not want to know that you handle administrative matters all day long. Instead, focus on the outcome or benefit: for example, that you spot errors in order forms that could otherwise cause customer dissatisfaction. As another example, do not simply write that you can build spreadsheets that incorporate complex macros. Again, focus on the benefit, for example that you once built a spreadsheet that helped the company to reduce costs by 8 per cent.

Second, think about the outcomes that you want to achieve in all of your work from now on. Rather than just getting on with your day-to-day job, ask yourself, is this work important and how does it benefit my organization? Focus on benefits that you would be able to talk about to other people. Prioritize and choose to work on tasks of greater importance. Otherwise, if you find yourself saying that your work is of little importance, it follows that your organization probably thinks that you are also of little importance.

Continuing professional and personal development

One of the most obvious ways of demonstrating your skills and experience is to take professional exams and pick up diplomas, certificates, degrees and other qualifications. Having a few added letters after your name is a clear signal to employers that you are a committed worker. And even if you plan to work for yourself in the future, qualifications will show prospective customers or clients that you are competent and credible in your chosen field.

Further qualifications are not restricted only to people who have had a university education. For example, Access courses are available to those who left school when they were perhaps only 14 or 15 years old. Mature students often do not require A-levels to get into university. Universities and learning establishments are increasingly offering a wider variety of courses. For example, if you would like to do a doctorate, the traditional full-time or part-time course typically involves attending a number of lectures or seminars as well as completing a piece of supervised research. However, a growing number of institutions offer executive doctorates, which allow people to gather research as part of their work, with only minimal contact with a course tutor perhaps once every few months. Similarly, business schools typically offer full-time or part-time MBA programmes that can last several years. However, they also frequently offer executive MBA programmes for people in a hurry who want only to dedicate maybe an intensive period of 12 to 16 weeks to the course.

Before embarking on a professional qualification, however, you should take yourself through the following list of questions:

▦ Why am I doing this course?

▦ How do employers view this course? Is it widely recognized outside of my field, or just by people within my field?

▦ Who is teaching the course and what is their reputation in the field?

▦ What modules or options are available to me on this course? Will I be motivated enough to survive the modules that I am not interested in?

- What doors does this course open up for me?
- But also, what doors might this course close? Is there a danger that future employers might view me as having specialized too much for other more general roles?
- What are the financial costs involved in taking this qualification?
- What sort of demands will I face in studying? Will I study and work at the same time?
- What sort of demands will my study put upon my partner or family and what practical support can I realistically expect from them?
- How is the course assessed (for example, essays, continuous assessment, group project work, end-of-year exams) and how do those methods suit me?

You should think of these many questions as an opportunity to work out whether any particular qualification really is right for you. However, there is no doubt that the right professional qualification can make a huge difference to your career. For example, salary surveys repeatedly confirm that people who are more qualified tend to earn more.

Personal development

This chapter has focused heavily on continuing professional development. However, employers do not look only for particular skills and experience. Often, you may not have the directly relevant skills or experience for the role. However, they may be willing to take you on if you can demonstrate a willingness and ability to pick up new skills quickly, and having non-work skills on your CV will help to demonstrate this aptitude for learning. It could be anything from taking up a musical instrument to cordon bleu cooking lessons, a new sport or physical activity, perhaps a foreign language or taking a leadership role in a charity or community group.

Non-work experiences can have an indirect bearing on your attractiveness to new employers too. At the end of the day, employers often use the so-called 'Pittsburgh Airport test'. Now, I have not been to Pittsburgh myself, so cannot claim to know it intimately. But ex-colleagues of mine from a large management consultancy used to say that Pittsburgh Airport was a very boring place, with little to do. When meeting candidates keen to join the firm, their question to themselves was always: 'If my flight got cancelled and I was stuck at Pittsburgh Airport for 24 hours with this person, how would I feel?'

Even if employers do not call it the Pittsburgh Airport test, they may often be asking themselves: 'Could I go for lunch, a drink or a long car journey with this person and enjoy it?' Consequently, when you do come to changing jobs, those new skills will give you more to talk about in such situations and therefore make you more attractive as a prospective employee than other candidates.

5

Jumping through organizational hoops

Organizations are associated with procedures and bureaucracy. As a rule, the larger the organization, the greater is the demand for form filling, process and bureaucracy. Even in companies with only a few dozen employees, the hoops in this chapter are still likely to apply to you.

Most of us just accept the fact that we must undergo these trials. However, this chapter looks at not only how to cope with them, but excel at them.

SELF-TEST: UNDERSTANDING YOUR ORGANIZATIONAL EFFECTIVENESS

The following questions may give you a sense of how good you currently are at making the most of the organizational hoops that you need to handle. Tick the statements that you agree with.

Table 5.1

	Tick
1. I make time to prepare before my appraisal	
2. I have an in-depth knowledge of internal training courses that are available to me	
3. I am ready to handle an exit interview when I resign from jobs	
4. I know what my performance objectives and targets are for the year	
5. My appraisals tend to focus on the future as opposed to my past performance	
6. I know how the internal interview process works for promotion	
7. I have a mentor within my company	
8. I know about the availability of external training courses and how to get on them	
9. I give my manager feedback on his or her performance during my appraisal	
10. I have a clear understanding of the targets I need to achieve for promotion	

Calculating your organizational effectiveness

Calculate your personal score simply by adding up the number of ticks.

Table 5.2

Your Score	Comment
0–4	You may be losing out because of your organizational naivety. Perhaps you expect your manager to provide everything on a plate for you. If you do not take action to pursue the training, mentoring, and internal opportunities that are available, you are at risk of being left to stagnate in your role.
5–8	You seem to have an average to good understanding of some of the opportunities and organizational processes that can help or hinder your career. But the fact that you did not score higher indicates that there is still some room for improvement. Read this chapter and identify the areas that you could work on.
9–10	You have an excellent appreciation of the organizational procedures that must be navigated. However, avoid letting yourself become complacent. You will need to keep an eye on how those procedures and processes change over time and adapt your own behaviour accordingly.

APPRAISALS

In theory, appraisals should be a chance for you to get feedback on your performance and help you think about your career aspirations and how to achieve them. More often than not, however, they focus on past performance rather than future plans, more of an end-of-term report than an opportunity to discuss career plans. In addition, managers are rarely trained or properly motivated to do them properly, and neither do appraisees do enough thinking and preparation for the event. If you think of your appraisal as a bureaucratic chore, you may be missing out on an opportunity to make a good impression on your manager, discuss new projects to keep you interested, and further your own career.

Preparation

Much of the work comes in a little forethought. Take time to:

- Recall your achievements over the months since your last appraisal. In particular, think of the skills that you have developed in those months. What have you learnt?

- Think back to mistakes you made or tasks that you felt you did not do well. Rather than wait for your manager to point out flaws in your performance, it is far more constructive for you to admit to your own faults. Were there genuine mitigating circumstances causing these flaws or mistakes? In addition, try to think about the learning points from those mistakes.

- Refer back to your previous appraisal. What were the expectations laid out in that appraisal and did you achieve them or not? If not, you need to think of a way to explain your failure as well as give confidence to your manager that you will achieve them in the coming months.

- Looking at both your achievements and mistakes, weigh up what training or type of projects you would like over the coming months to develop your skills. Are there courses that you could go on? Would working closely with another colleague help to enhance your skills in a particular area? Is there any support that you would like from your manager? Think also about the timescales for any training or development: is it something that could happen over a period of only a few weeks or does it require many months?

▧ In suggesting to your manger that you need to be sent on a training course that costs money, try to think of the benefits that it will achieve for the team or organization. Talking only about the benefits for you is a much less compelling argument. For example, think of time efficiencies or ways that you would be able to help other members of the team.

Handling the meeting

If you invest time in thinking beforehand, the meeting itself should be much more straightforward. However, do be assertive about what you want to say. If you do not agree with your manager's opinion, then do not just sit there and accept his or her criticism or observations.

Handling covert criticism

Most appraisals will involve some degree of criticism from your manager. However, few managers will choose to criticize you overtly; it is much easier for them to adopt the more insidious tactic of making 'observations' with covert value judgements behind these so-called observations. So you need to be alert in order to contest these veiled criticisms:

1. Listen to what your manager has to say. Even if you do not agree, give your manager the opportunity to finish rather than interrupting him or her, which can make the situation appear more confrontational than it needs to be.

2. If you agree with the criticism, then you need to accept it, perhaps offer an apology, and then move towards suggesting ways of improving your performance.

3. If you do not agree with the criticism, you must first respond by accepting that the manager is allowed to have his or her own opinion.

4. Then think through what you do not agree with. Do you not understand what the manager is trying to say? If not, perhaps you could ask for examples of when you allegedly behaved in the unacceptable fashion.

5. Alternatively, if you understand the situations that the manager is referring to, you should put your point of view across. Perhaps there were extenuating circumstances that you need to explain. Or perhaps your manager had misinterpreted or exaggerated a particular situation.

6. Whatever the discussion, make sure that you work towards agreeing how you will behave in the future. A useful way to check that you are on the right road to improving your performance is to suggest to your manager that you meet up again in, say three or four months, as opposed to waiting until your next annual appraisal. In this way, you can get some interim feedback on how well you are improving (or not).

Giving upward feedback

Use your appraisal as a formal opportunity to give some feedback on your manager's management of you. This needs to be done sensitively. One approach to giving constructive upward feedback is to talk about:

1. What do you like about your manager's management style? What would you like your manager to continue with? Giving your manager some positive strokes will make the negative feedback easier to take.

2. What do you not like about your manager's style of management? However, also think about a good reason why his or her style is not appropriate. It is not enough to say, 'I don't like it.' Try to think about the impact it has on your

work: for example, 'The fact that you keep checking up on me several times a day means that it takes me a lot longer to get the job done.'

3. Finally, how would you like your manager to behave differently? Come up with a solution as opposed to just complaining. So, rather than saying, 'I don't want you to check up on me so often,' perhaps, 'After you give me a task, I would rather report back to you once a day at an agreed time.' And again try to point out the benefits for your manager: 'This would mean that I could get the work done more quickly for you.'

PROMOTION

If you want to get promoted, the most important lesson to learn is that being good at your job is not enough on its own to guarantee you a promotion. Getting a promotion involves at least three essential elements: competence, confidence, and a compelling argument.

Competence

It *should* go without saying, but unfortunately people can occasionally overlook the fact that before you can be promoted to a new role with additional responsibilities, you need to be sure that you are performing competently at your current role. Take a hard look at your current performance. Are there any areas at all in which your performance could receive criticism? If so, there is no point in trying to get a promotion. Chapter 7 may provide some ideas for identifying areas for improvement.

Once you are sure that you are performing your current job competently, you need to begin to exhibit the behaviours that are required of the role that you want. If there is a job description that outlines the requirements of the role that you would like to be promoted to, you need to understand this thoroughly. A good job description may also mention the competencies or skills that are required of the new role. Typically, organizations are looking for people who can motivate members of the team to deliver customer service and/or boost revenues and profits. Is there any way that you can begin to change your behaviour to show some of those new skills?

Confidence

The next step is to put yourself in the shoes of the people who can make the decision whether to promote you or not. The key here is to give them confidence that you can do the job. Quite often, senior managers have an idea of how newly promoted people should behave; they are looking for people who can 'walk the talk'.

Look around the organization at the people who are already doing the job that you want. If there are no incumbents in exactly the same job, then look around at the next level of supervisor or manager above you, perhaps in other departments. What sort of work or projects do they get involved in? What day-to-day activities do they engage in? Is there anything in their behaviour that marks them out as different from the people that they manage? For example, are there any technical skills that the role requires, or does the role require a shift from doing work to delegating work to others?

Chapter 6 may also give you some insight into management. Once you understand the answers to some of these questions, you can begin to pick up these new skills with the aim of impressing the decision-makers. Focus on what you will need to do differently, and focus on getting yourself noticed for these new skills.

Compelling argument

The third essential element is a way to persuade the decision-makers that you are right for the job. At the beginning of the section, I mentioned that doing a good job is not necessarily enough to gain you a promotion. You need to make the decision-makers aware of your desire to be promoted. There are many people who enjoy doing the job that they currently do and do not wish to have the stress that might go with a promotion. So unless you make yourself heard, how else can the decision-makers distinguish you from someone who is entirely content in his or her current role?

Consequently, identify the key decision-maker. It may not be your boss, but perhaps your boss's boss or the head of a different department entirely. Then go to that person and make your case, presenting evidence of your good work in recent months.

Timing

There is a fourth element to being promoted, and one you have little control over. Even though you may have the right skills and motivation, there are often only limited opportunities for promotion. So there is an element of luck and timing in achieving a promotion as well. For example, an organization in the middle of a cost-cutting programme is unlikely to be looking to promote people when it might be trying to make people redundant. Or there may simply not be any positions available because of a lack of movement in the hierarchies above you. If this is the case, you have two options. Either you can wait it out for a vacancy to arise within your organization, or you could consider options in other companies. Exactly how much do you want a promotion?

INTERNAL INTERVIEWS AND ASSESSMENT CENTRES

When you are putting yourself forward for promotion, some organizations have a policy of recruiting from within, so there might be other internal candidates for the job. Other organizations will advertise jobs in the press or place the vacancy with recruitment consultants as a matter of course, potentially bringing in external candidates. In either case, the decision-makers typically will put all the candidates through an interview or assessment process to choose the best candidate.

Such selection processes can vary hugely. Your job as a candidate is to understand the process as well as you can beforehand. While some organizations might have a number of one-to-one interviews, another organization might put candidates through an extensive assessment process comprising business case simulations, role play simulations, presentations and psychometric tests. Try to find out as much information as possible about the selection process. Some questions to ask are:

▮ What are the different stages of the selection process? Will there be multiple rounds of interviews or just one?

▮ If there is an assessment process, where will it be held? Will it be held in the usual workplace or elsewhere, perhaps a hotel or conference centre?

▮ Will external interviewers or assessors be involved in the selection process? If so, try to get access to their corporate literature or Web site beforehand, as these often have information on their philosophy and style of interviewing or assessment.

▮ How many other candidates are there for the role? Will all of the candidates meet and interact with each other during any assessment process?

While you may not be allowed inside information as to the exact nature of the exercises involved, having more information beforehand will at least help you to relax and perform to the best of your ability on the day.

Coping with failure

If you fail to emerge as the favoured candidate, you must ask for feedback as to why you were not selected. The decision-makers might tell you that 'another candidate was stronger'. However, you should not allow them to fob you off so easily. Ideally, set up a face-to-face meeting – or at minimum book an appointment for a proper telephone conversation – to understand exactly why you were not chosen. Then take on board the feedback and think about how you will improve yourself for the next time a promotion opportunity arises.

Dealing with success

When you do eventually achieve that promotion, you might be tempted to sit back and congratulate yourself. Before you do so, however, take a look at Chapter 9 on negotiating a good deal. Many employers imply that there is a set amount of pay and benefits for a particular grade or level. In reality, however, there is often some scope for discussion.

TRAINING COURSES

Some employers offer internal training courses – perhaps run by the HR department – on topics such as time management, presentation skills and leadership development. Other departments might also offer more specialized training courses in legal affairs, health and safety, or IT skills.

However, it is dangerous to assume that the 'powers that be' – in other words your manager and the other managers in the organization – will automatically have your best interests at heart and encourage you to go on the right courses. Many organizations have a training budget for employee development, but then keep quiet about it in the hopes of saving the money. Even though most organizations talk about the importance of developing their most important assets – allegedly their employees – they sometimes need to be reminded to do so.

As a matter of course, you should keep an eye out for the training courses, seminars or development programmes that might be available to you. If your organization is large enough, you should:

∎ Get to know the HR manager or administrator allocated to look after your team, department, division or business unit. Get to know this individual and use him or her as a sounding board for your career aspirations. If you want to move in a particular career direction, then ask the HR person whether there are any internal courses that you could go on.

∎ Use your appraisal as an opportunity to raise the issue of your development with your manager. However, you might need to persuade your manager with a convincing argument about the benefits of the course.

External courses

If you do not work in a company that is large enough to offer its own in-house training courses, you will need to look externally to find courses to develop your skills. However, even if you do work for a large enough employer that does offer in-house skills courses, you may sometimes need to look externally for a course or programme that better fits your particular needs. Often, you will find that what is available internally does not suit your specific needs: perhaps it is either too basic or too advanced.

However, external courses tend to be more expensive than internal courses, so your arguments will need to be even more compelling. It might be worth writing a business case to present to your manager, as a carefully researched and well-written document is far more likely to convince a manager than a hurried and ill-prepared discussion. You might wish to answer the following questions in your business case:

∎ Why do you need to go on a course at all? What skill gap or need does it fill?

∎ What benefits would you gain from it?

∎ What benefits would there be for the rest of the team, your manager, or the organization in general?

∎ Why can other methods – such as work shadowing or having other colleagues sit with you – not help to fill in the skill gap?

- How much will the external course cost? Would there be overnight accommodation costs as well? Depending on how important the course is to you, would you be willing to shoulder some of the fees yourself?

- How many days would you be away from the office for? And how would you arrange cover while you are away?

- What other external options are there? If you present your manager with just one course, he or she must effectively make a binary decision, saying either 'yes' or 'no' to your request. However, if you present a few courses – perhaps a lengthy and more expensive one as well as a less expensive and shorter course that delivers 80 per cent of the benefit – your manager might be more inclined to accede to your request in some form.

When considering external courses you might also want to refer to Chapter 4, which contains further questions that you need to be able to answer to your own satisfaction.

MENTORING

Few organizations provide an official mentoring scheme for employees. Even at senior management levels, organizations typically expect an individual's line manager to act as coach and mentor for them. However, the benefits of having an additional mentor who is not your direct manager include:

- Being able to talk about political issues within your team. Sometimes, you might not feel able to raise these with your manager because such issues within a team could by implication be criticizing your manager's leadership of the team.

- Having a sounding board for any difficulties that you might be experiencing.

▪ Gaining a fresh perspective on long-term career opportunities that you might not be able to see for yourself because you are too busy coping with the day-to-day work.

▪ Having someone to talk to when the problem is your manager.

Finding a mentor

When choosing a mentor within your organization, it is important to think about their qualities as well as their qualifications. The most important quality is that your mentor should be someone that you can trust to help you in your career. You should be able to talk to him or her candidly about issues and difficulties without feeling that he or she is then going to go either to your manager or other colleagues behind your back. In addition, a good mentor should ideally have good listening skills and an ability to tell you what you might not want to hear. Your mentor is not there to be your best friend but to help you develop in your career. You probably have enough friends who can provide you with sympathy and support; but what a mentor can do is challenge you and bring to your attention issues that you might not wish to admit to yourself.

In choosing a mentor, you should spend a good amount of time evaluating prospective mentors. Who can you trust not to talk behind your back? And do you believe that he or she could talk to you in a direct manner that borders on tactlessness, perhaps pointing out the rough edges in your personality or stripping away the excuses and rationalizations that we can all use to defend how we behave?

Approaching prospective mentors

The following points might help you to choose a mentor effectively:

1. Think about how you will approach your prospective mentor. You might be wondering why another individual

would want to mentor you. However, the truth of the matter is that most people, when asked to mentor someone else, actually feel flattered. Imagine if someone a bit more junior than yourself came to you and asked you for your advice, your straightforward manner, and the benefit of your experience in developing his or her career; you would probably feel delighted to have been asked.

2. If an individual turns down your mentoring request, then ask why he or she is turning you down. For example, he or she might worry that he/she does not know your team well enough, in which case you could counter by saying that he/she does not need to know your team. You want this person to be your mentor because you trust him or her and value his/her candour. Perhaps the person feels that he or she does not have enough time, in which case you could suggest that you meet only very infrequently, say once every six months, or perhaps over a lunch that you would buy.

3. Do have a few possible candidates for acting as your mentor. Some of the people you ask might just be too busy or fail to see the benefit (to them) of mentoring you.

4. When an individual finally agrees to be your mentor, you need to agree the frequency and duration of each session. How often will you meet? And how much time does the mentor feel able to commit to each mentoring session? For example, will you meet for an hour every two months or a few hours every quarter?

5. Think about other practical issues. Where will you meet? Is it okay to meet in his or her office? Or would it be better for either or both of you if the meeting could take place away from prying ears and eyes?

6. Also consider how you will use each session. You do not want to waste your mentor's time by having a general chat about nothing in particular. You need to structure the time so that the mentor feels that each mentoring session is worth-

while. Perhaps you need to spend half an hour before each mentoring session to think about the current problems you are facing that your mentor could help you with. Avoid bothering your mentor with inconsequential matters or day-to-day problems. Instead, use your mentor to give you advice on the more intractable problems or career dilemmas that you might be facing.

There are also arguments for having a mentor outside your organization. This is particularly common when an individual works in a small organization of perhaps only a few dozen people. With so few people to choose from, you might think that there is no one else qualified within the organization, or you might feel that you simply do not have a good enough rapport and trusting relationship with anyone else. In such cases, it might be a good idea to broaden your search externally. Even if you cannot think of anyone off the top of your head, you might come up with a few suitable candidates after reading Chapter 11 on the topic of networking.

RESIGNING

Over the course of your working life, you might find the need to move perhaps several times in your efforts to secure more pay, better opportunities, less stress or whatever else you are looking for in your career. No matter how much you disliked your colleagues, hated the work, or detested your boss, it never pays to leave on bad terms with an employer. For a start, you never know when you might need a reference in the future. The people at a previous employer can often form an important part of your network (see Chapter 11). And should the worse come to the worst and a new job or business venture should go sour, resigning on good terms makes it easier for you to ask for your old job back.

Before we think about how to resign with good grace, let us think about how not to resign. First, you should never *threaten* to resign. People who threaten to resign often believe that it is a bargaining tactic; they hope that their boss will see their value and beg for them to stay, offering better working conditions, promotions or whatever else they want. However, the reality is often very different. Bosses often have large egos that make it extremely difficult for them to acknowledge other people. Even if you are invaluable, they might feel obliged not to show how much they need you. If you threaten to resign, you could easily find your boss accepting it on the spot.

Similarly, avoid resigning when you are angry. Often, when you are feeling calmer, the situation will seem completely different. If you do threaten to resign, or resign, when you are angry, you might end up backed into a corner. You could end up being either forced to resign and having nothing better to go to, or forced into issuing a humiliating retraction.

If you are thinking of resigning, consider the following points:

∎ Always ensure that you have something better to do. That 'something' could be a firm offer from a company that you feel will offer you the right career opportunities. Or perhaps you have already taken steps to set up your own business and now feel that the time is right to work for yourself full-time.

∎ Think about how you will explain why you are leaving to your boss. No one says that you have to be entirely honest. Focus on the positive attractions of your new career choice as opposed to whining about the negative points of your current job.

∎ If you do want to mention any negative points about your current job, then at least keep it professional: never personal. Talk about professional issues such as limited opportunities, bureaucracy or other issues, but not clashes with your manager or other difficult individuals.

■ Bear in mind that your employer might make a counter offer. If he or she did offer you more money, more interesting work or whatever else you say you are looking for in your new job, would you consider staying? Ask yourself why it took the threat of resigning to force your employer into recognizing your worth. Do you *believe* that the employer can really deal with the issues that are making you leave?

People are divided as to whether it is better to write a formal letter and hand that in or to have an informal discussion with your manager first. There is no 'right answer'. However, many people find that it helps them to get their thoughts together by writing a resignation letter and then handing it personally to their boss, perhaps saying at the same time, 'I've decided to resign, but I wanted to tell you in person.'

Exit interviews

Many employers have one final organizational hoop for employees to jump through: the exit interview. The idea behind an exit interview is to establish what the organization could be doing better. Best practice dictates that exit interviews should be conducted by an impartial third party, perhaps by HR or a colleague from another department who does not have an axe to grind with you. On occasion, however, an exit interview could be performed by your manager, making it even more perilous for you to be too honest.

If you are expecting to have to participate in an exit interview, the secret to passing it with flying colours is much the same as handling your resignation:

■ Have in mind a story to tell about the positive aspects of the new career choice that you are making.

■ Rehearse a few careful comments on what you did not like about the organization. The interviewer is likely to ask you specifically what was wrong with the organization. Be critical, but constructive; be impersonal rather than personal. One tactic is to focus on ineffective systems and processes rather than mentioning people problems. An alternative might be to talk about the clash between departments – perhaps the constant tension between the sales department and finance – rather than the clash between individuals.

◾ Finally, think what was good about your organization. Emphasize the qualities that make it difficult for you to leave. In this way, you will maintain good relations with your former employer, paving the way should you ever need to return to them for a reference, advice or information, or even your old job.

6

Moving up in management

If you want more from your career such as more responsibility, more opportunities, or more pay and benefits, you will eventually need to move into management. There is a big difference between being a good team worker and a good team manager. Being a manager means being accountable for other people: making choices on behalf of your team, understanding their individual strengths and identifying ways of getting the best out of them, and even firing them if they under-perform. Have you got what it takes?

Or if you are already managing others but have aspirations of rising higher within the ranks of management, you may need to take a keen look at how you manage. Are you a lacklustre manager or a valued leader?

SELF-TEST: MEASURING YOUR READINESS FOR MANAGEMENT

The following is a quiz designed for people who are not currently in management. If you are already in a supervisory or management role you can skip this quiz, as you clearly have decided to embark on the route of management. However, if you are not yet a manager, this may help you to identify whether you have the aptitude as well as the attitude necessary to make it in management. Before presuming to manage other people, you must first make sure that you can manage yourself.

Read the list of statements and then decide whether you agree, disagree, or have no particular feelings about each one. Some of the statements are about your current and past behaviour and experiences, while a few of the statements are asking you for your opinions about management. As with all of these question-naires, only honesty will give you a useful analysis of your readiness for management.

Table 6.1

	Agree	Unsure	Disagree
1. My colleagues would agree that I am someone who applauds good work frequently			
2. At school and/or university, I sought out positions of leadership such as team captain, school prefect, society president			
3. I have excellent relationships with all of my peers			
4. I don't mind telling people that they have done a bad job of something			
5. I can think of many occasions when I have patiently explained something to another person			
6. I can concede a point gracefully when I am in the wrong			
7. I try to relate what I am doing in my work to the organization's overall goals			
8. I would go so far as to say that my boss is a good role model for me			
9. I would reward hard work (but poor results) as well as good results themselves			
10. Even when I know that I am right, I sometimes concede the point because good relationships are more important than being proved right			
11. I think that employees should be encouraged to challenge the decisions of their boss			
12. I don't mind it when other people take credit for my achievements			

Interpreting your management readiness score

To calculate your management readiness score, add up your score as follows:

▪ −1 point every time you chose to disagree with the statement.

▪ 0 points every time you were unsure about the statement.

▪ +2 points every time you chose to agree with the statement.

Table 6.2

Your score	
8 or under	At this point in time, it seems that you may be far from ready to adopt responsibility for other people. You do not seem to enjoy explaining matters to other people or applauding their good work. If you really do want to be a manager in the future, you will need to invest serious effort into changing yourself. Chapter 7 may help you to understand your current weaknesses and give you ideas on how to change the way that you are.
9–18	You may not be entirely ready to take on the mantle of becoming a manager yet. However, you are far from a lost cause. There are likely to be a few areas that you need to work on. Chapter 7 will help you to fine-tune some of these skills to prepare you for management.
19–23	You seem to have the attitude and perhaps some of the aptitude for becoming a manager. The next step is simply to go for it!
24 points	You are either perfect material for a manager or deluding yourself. Are you sure that you answered all of the questions with complete honesty?

FROM TEAM *WORKER* TO TEAM *MANAGER*

There is insufficient space to write in much depth on the topic of what makes a good manager. Whole books are dedicated to the skills that are required. Rather than talking about these many skills (delegating, setting targets, motivating, handling disciplinary matters, communicating, resolving conflict, the list goes on and on), we shall only cover five basic principles, which are based heavily on surveys of what employees want from their managers.

You may be wondering, what use are only five principles when managing a team requires so many skills? Well, these principles should provide a framework for all of the decisions that you make as a manager. Rather than providing you with the minutiae of becoming a manager, these five principles should inform all your thinking. If you keep these principles in mind at all times, you will pick up the other skills with time. Think of these as the five commandments of managing effectively. If you try to apply these principles to the many skills and situations that you face, you are unlikely to go far wrong.

Seek input from your team

In surveys, employees frequently complain about managers who have 'poor communication' skills. When asked what they mean by this, they often say that their manager refuses to listen to their ideas. As a manager, you may feel that the burden of responsibility should fall on you to make decisions. However, most teams would love to be involved in making the decisions with you.

Becoming a manager might mean that you become more remote from your customers, so you must rely on the eyes and ears of your team to report back to you what customers want. Your team will have input and ideas. Sometimes their ideas may not have been well thought-through or practicable in a situation, but at other times they could provide a solution that you had not considered before. For example, I worked with a manager who had been told that he needed to cut costs in his team by 20 per cent. Initially he thought that this would involve making a few members of his team redundant. However, he told his team the situation and asked for their input. After some lengthy brainstorming, they came up with an idea to sublet some of their branch office space. To cut a long story short, they managed to reduce their costs without making a single person redundant, thereby keeping the morale of the team high.

Giving your team the opportunity to get involved will gain their commitment and 'buy in' to whatever final decision is taken. And to invite their suggestions, all you need to do is ask: 'What do you think?'

Trust your team

Seeking the input of your team is important, but you also need to be able to trust them. As a manager, it is easy to fall into the trap of seeking their input into a decision, and then simply issuing them with clear instructions as to what they each need to do. However, for a member of the team it is not always very motivating to have instructions given to you all of the time. Feeling like just a pair of hands is not good. Indeed, one of the most common complaints employees have about their managers is that they hate being 'micro-managed'.

Try giving members of your team some latitude in how they complete the task. Rather than spelling out the details of the task, give each member of your team the opportunity to use his or her brains. It is fine for you to focus on the end result, but you should allow members of your team to find an approach that works for them. Consider a hypothetical example: you need to ask a member of your team to research how much it would cost to update the computers in your department. One member of your team might prefer to begin by looking on the Internet for prices and information and speaking to ex-colleagues in other companies for advice; another individual might prefer to go straight to potential suppliers for quotes. However, the results of either approach are likely to be broadly the same.

Of course, you need to watch out that you do not go to the far extreme of leaving people in your team entirely on their own, with no coaching or support from you, as this is not delegation but abdication of responsibility. But at the end of the day, employees who feel trusted enough to be left alone to do their work will thank you for it.

Make decisions transparent

The first principle discussed the importance of seeking input into decisions. However, there are often situations where it is either not possible – perhaps due to a lack of time – or appropriate to talk to your team first. For example, an emergency may necessitate your barking orders at people to get the job done quickly, or perhaps you have sensitive information that should not be shared widely, such as evidence of gross misconduct from one of the members of your team which means that you will have to fire the individual.

When you do have to make such decisions, though, you need to explain the reasons for your decision as quickly as possible. For example, when mediating conflicts between members of your team, you obviously need to listen to the different parties before making your decision, but then go on to explain your reasoning. It can be easy to assume that the rationale for your decision is clear enough, because it is clear in your mind. But when people are locked in a dispute with each other, they might not have your clarity unless you explain it to them.

In situations when it is not appropriate to share all of the details, you still need to share as much as you can. Otherwise, the grapevine will start to spread rumours about why you may have taken the decision: and the grapevine is rarely boss-friendly. However, ensuring that you are as transparent as you can be, by explaining your reasons after the fact, is as effective as pouring weed-killer on the grapevine.

Recognize effort, reward results

People do not just work for money. In fact, surveys repeatedly show that what keeps them in one organization (as opposed to doing the same or a similar job in another organization) is a feeling of being appreciated for the work that they do.

People expect to be rewarded for delivering results. Rewards can come in a variety of forms, although most employees think of pay and bonuses as the ultimate rewards. However, rewards are only effective if members of the team know ahead of time what they need to deliver in order to receive them. Of course, with only limited resources you cannot heap rewards on members of your team all of the time. Good work has to be over a period of time rather than in bursts; and the people who perform the best must necessarily get better rewards than those who only perform adequately.

However, members of your team deserve acknowledgment for more than just results. Praise and compliments should also be used to recognize effort and hard work. Feeling competent and having a sense of achievement about one's work is a major motivator that team members frequently cite as to why they enjoy their working for one manager as opposed to another.

Be a role model

You may have heard some managers throw phrases around like 'walk the talk' and 'live the values'. These are essentially saying that good managers should behave in a way that is consistent with what they instruct others to do.

You may think that this principle is common sense, but you would be surprised how many team members complain that their manager unwittingly gives out the message, 'Do as I say, not as I do.' For example, if you are trying to promote a culture of greater customer focus, then make sure that you personally talk to customers occasionally. If you want to foster better collaboration and teamwork, then do not make flippant or cynical comments about your fellow managers. Or if you are going to point out certain flaws in your team, make sure that you are not guilty of making the same mistakes.

Again, this is a principle that should influence how you behave at all times at work. It is human nature for the members of your team to more readily notice your lapses than recognize your good points. Your team members are watching and listening, and be certain that evidence of any bad behaviour spreads very quickly on the grapevine. It is a difficult principle to live up to, but the danger of not being a good role model is that you will lose all credibility with your team.

Bringing the five principles together

Taking these five principles together, it would almost be possible to summarize them as one super-principle: *treat your team fairly and gain their respect*. If your team enjoys working for you and respects your decisions, then they will bend over backwards to do well. Employees would much rather work for a well-meaning but occasionally inept manager than one who is skilful but loathsome.

SELF-TEST: DISTINGUISHING LEADERSHIP FROM MANAGERSHIP

This questionnaire is aimed at helping people who are *currently* managers to think about how they can ascend the ranks of middle and senior management. There is little point completing this test unless you are actually managing a team; it is far better to save it until you have managed a team for at least six months or so.

Some people say, 'I don't need to be a leader,' assuming that you only need leadership skills to be a chief executive or public figure. But even if you only have a team of several people these are the skills that will help to make you stand out from your peers.

Before we discuss what the difference is between leadership and managership – and also the reasons why it is an important distinction – the following quiz will help you to identify your current style. Be honest with yourself as you decide the extent to which you agree or disagree with each of the following sixteen statements.

Table 6.3

	Agree	Unsure	Disagree
1. I am good at managing the day-to-day performance of my team			
2. I let the team know how they contribute to the organization's strategic goals			
3. I focus on clear short-term goals (over days or weeks) for the team to achieve			
4. I am able to articulate a clear vision for my team			
5. I always get appraisals done on time for my team			
6. I have invested energy in developing a successor to replace me			
7. I have a good understanding of the strengths and weaknesses of each member of my team			
8. I can communicate a sense of excitement over future possibilities			
9. I check up on members of my team to ensure that they are not struggling with their work			
10. I look for ways of sharing ideas with departments outside of my own			
11. I confront members of my team who are habitually bad with their time keeping			
12. I know what members of my team would each like to be doing in five years' time			
13. I know on a day-to-day basis how our team is performing against our weekly or monthly targets			
14. I focus on clear long-term goals (over many months) for the team to achieve			
15. I am good at breaking down complex tasks into clear roles and responsibilities for my team			
16. I encourage members of the team to pursue their own personal goals			

Calculating your managership versus leadership

Add up your managership score as follows:

- Award yourself 1 point each time you agreed with the odd numbered statements: 1, 3, 5, 7, 9, 11, 13 and 15.
- Subtract 1 point each time you disagreed with any of the odd numbered statements.

Now calculate your leadership score as follows:

- Add 1 point every time you agreed with the even numbered statements: 2, 4, 6, 8, 10, 12, 14 and 16.
- Subtract 1 point every time you disagreed with each of the even numbered statements.

Table 6.4

Write your managership score here	Write your leadership score here

These two scores for managership and leadership should give you an idea of where you focus your time and energy. Unlike many of the self-test questionnaires in this book, however, having a much higher score on either managership or leadership is not a good thing. It may mean that you are focusing on one set of behaviours at the neglect of the other. If your score on one was much higher than the other, then you need to think about how you could redress the balance (a topic that is touched upon in Chapter 7). A good manager should focus on both the tasks of managership and leadership: a score of 7 or 8 on both scales would indicate that you are doing a good job. Anything less may indicate that more effort is required.

Understanding managership

Managership is about dealing with the day-to-day or week-to-week tasks of running a team effectively. There are organizational rules that need to be followed, such as legal requirements or guidelines governing health and safety. There are processes that need to be adhered to, such as filling out forms for annual leave and absenteeism. Performance management – that is, dealing with issues such as completing appraisals and taking disciplinary action – also falls under the category of managership.

There might also be monthly, weekly, or even daily targets that need to be met. For example, if you were the manager of a call centre, you would need to keep track of how many callers are waiting in a queue at any time and take appropriate action to ensure that callers are not waiting for too long.

Good managership is therefore about dealing with organizational systems, structures and processes. By following the rules, a manager seeks to create order and minimize risks. It is about coming up with tactics for delivering short-term results that meet the organization's needs.

Understanding leadership

There used to be a belief that 'leaders are born, not made', but more recent studies show that leadership is a skill that can be developed. Leadership is in many ways the opposite of managership. Leadership is not focused on the mundane aspects of getting the day-to-day work done. It is about having a vision, a 'big picture' idea of where the organization should be going in the future: a future that may have a timescale of years as opposed to months. Leadership is about articulating and communicating that vision, speaking passionately and painting a vivid picture about future possibilities that inspires and excites people.

A vision may challenge existing organizational rules, bureaucracy and accepted thinking. The vision may sound like 'pie in the sky', but a pie that might just be reachable with hard work. For example, rather than thinking about serving current customers better, a vision asks who will be the organization's future customers in say five or 10 years' time. Or a vision might try to tackle grand issues such as how technology or social change might affect demand for the organization's products and services. A vision should also raise questions about the type of people that the organization should employ, and the skills that they will need to meet these future demands.

Good leadership is therefore to do with thinking about the long-term future of the organization. It is about tolerating uncertainty and taking measured risks. So, rather than simply keeping things ticking over, how can the organization transform itself to continue being successful?

COMBINING MANAGERSHIP WITH LEADERSHIP

What the questionnaires and brief discussion should highlight is the importance of both sets of skills to manage effectively. Neither managership nor leadership is sufficient on its own.

Consider an individual manager who has strong managership skills but lacks leadership. Such a manager would be good at focusing on day-to-day tasks. Colleagues and senior managers might trust such a manager as a 'safe pair of hands' for motivating a team to achieve short-term results. However, managers at the top of the organization may feel that the individual is not sufficiently strategic: that the individual lacks the ability to inspire and think about the big changes that will help the organization to prosper in the long-term. They might view the individual as more of a supervisor than a leader: a view that is almost certain to hold the individual's career back.

On the other hand, let us consider the individual who is gifted in leadership but fails to focus on managership. This sort of person may be recognized, by peers and bosses alike as an inspiring individual with impressive ideas for the future. However, lack of ability or perhaps lack of attention to day-to-day matters may make the individual an unreliable manager, leading to frustration in colleagues and customers alike. Without the ability to deliver short-term goals, colleagues may doubt the manager's ability to turn the vision into reality. The manager's vision could end up sounding like empty rhetoric. Again, the people at the top are unlikely to give much responsibility to this kind of manager.

To sum up, both of these skills are necessary if you really want to move up in management.

EXERCISE: LEARNING FROM ROLE MODELS

Being an effective manager and a good leader involves a set of behaviours and qualities that is hard to define. Leadership is also heavily influenced by the culture of a particular organization. In order to help you to pick up the right skills and qualities for your organization, try the following exercise:

- Think about three managers in your organization who are widely admired by you and your colleagues. Talk to your colleagues and try to find out why each of these managers is held in regard. Ask your colleagues, what qualities do these managers have? And what is it that they say or do that makes them good managers?

- Observe these managers, if you can, over the course of several weeks. It helps some people after each session of observation to write down a few notes on particular phrases that a respected manager uses. Or you might want to take mental note of their personal style or techniques that you see them using.

▮ Finally, think about what you can learn from your observations. Is there anything that you could adapt for use with your own team to be a better leader?

7

Understanding your impact on others

In my work as a career coach and mentor, I often work with individuals who feel that they are not being given the recognition
they deserve. However, when we delve into the situation a little
more, we often discover that there is a mismatch between what
the individuals think of themselves and what their colleagues
think of them.

The point is that perception often rules over reality. For
example, you might see yourself as an individual who is
confident and honest, while others might perceive you to be
arrogant and tactless. Perhaps you feel that you are a trusting
person, but others see you as a gullible person to be taken
advantage of. Or you might think of yourself as spontaneous and
easy-going, while others may perceive you as being disorganized.

Perception often rules over reality in the many situations that
we encounter as well. Consider a hypothetical situation in which
you have an argument with a customer. You might have been in

the right and the customer in the wrong. But the customer then complains to your boss before you can speak to your boss. Unfortunately, by the time you get the opportunity to speak to your boss, he or she might already have made up their mind about the situation. They might make an effort to listen to your side of the story, yet still take action against you. Again, your boss's perception of the situation has overruled the reality of the situation.

However, psychologists have for years used personality inventories or 'tests' to help us understand how we behave and therefore also how we could come across to others. The Myers-Briggs Type Indicator (MBTI) is one of the most commonly used personality tools in the workplace, in both the private and public sectors. For example, the MBTI is frequently taught to managers on leadership development courses. This chapter will help you to understand your personality and how it might affect how others perceive you.

SELF-TEST: UNDERSTANDING YOUR PERSONALITY TYPE

Originally based on Jungian theory, the MBTI describes our natural preferences on four dimensions of personality. For reasons of copyright, the questions in this chapter do not constitute the full questionnaire. So these questions will only be able to give you an approximate feel for your MBTI profile.

Administering the full version of the MBTI is something that only chartered psychologists – such as my colleagues and I at Kiddy and Partners – should do. So if, at the end of completing this quick test, you feel that you need a more in-depth understanding of your MBTI profile, you should get in touch with a chartered psychologist: perhaps through the British Psychological Society or the Association of Business Psychologists.

Once that has been said, though, these next four sections and the brief analysis below should give you an excellent introduction to your personality.

Extroversion versus introversion

Before we look at what these two terms mean, just take a few minutes to complete the quick test. Look at the following pairs of statements and put a tick in *either* column E or column I, depending on which statement or adjective you think describes you best.

Table 7.1

Column E	Column I
Blurting it out	Keeping it in
Interaction with others	Time on my own to think
Liking a buzz of colleagues around you	Liking space to think by myself
Taking action now	Thinking about it first
Talking it over	Mulling it over
Speaking my mind	Waiting and seeing
Having a breadth of interests	Having a depth of interests

Now simply total up the number of ticks for column E, then do the same for column I. Whichever is your highest score describes whether you are an extrovert or an introvert. However, being an extrovert or an introvert is not as much of a black and white situation as the quiz may imply. In reality, the extroversion–introversion dimension is a sliding scale, with some people being strong extroverts or introverts, while others may only be slightly extroverted or introverted. The bigger the difference between your E score and I score, the stronger you are likely to be one or the other. On the other hand, if there is only one point between your E score and I score, you may sit in the middle of the extroversion–introversion scale.

Understanding extroversion/introversion

Extroversion and introversion do not refer to whether you have social skills or not. This is a common misconception as to whether you are the kind of person who has lots of friends or the kind of person who is deeply unpopular and shunned by all. The technical MBTI explanation of extroversion versus introversion refers to where you prefer to get your energy.

Extroverts like to draw their energy from the people around them; they like to take action and interact with the world and other people. They like to discuss ideas with other people and enjoy pace and activity. They pick up skills by trying them out, making mistakes, and learning from them.

Introverts, on the other hand, prefer the 'inner world' of concepts and ideas; they enjoy reflecting on their own. They do not mind having to work on their own, and they tend to pick up new skills by reading and thinking about them.

Neither type is better than the other, as each has its own particular strengths and weaknesses. By understanding the weaknesses associated with your particular personality type, you should hopefully be able to adapt your behaviour to make the right impression all of the time with the people that you deal with.

Table 7.2

	Extroverts	Introverts
Strengths	Enthusiastic manner Recognized by others as stimulating company Outspoken with their ideas Good team leaders	Able to come up with ideas on their own Good concentration and focus on their work Handling routine tasks that need doing Strong ability to work independently
Weaknesses	Find it difficult to come up with ideas on their own Get bored quickly Can often act quickly, sometimes without thinking through the consequences Tend to disappoint at tasks that require solitude and concentration	Find it difficult to concentrate with people around them May be too self-effacing and therefore can risk being undervalued by others Can get stressed by too many things happening at once Can appear aloof or unfriendly

Intuitive versus sensing

Again, before we look at what these two terms mean, take a few minutes to complete the quick quiz. Pick only one from each pair of statements and put a tick in *either* column N or column S, depending on the statement or adjective you think describes you best.

Table 7.3

Column N	Column S
Being theoretical	Being practical
Driven by concepts	Driven by detail
Making decisions based on what might work in the future	Making decisions based on what has worked before
Abstract	Concrete
Looking for insights	Looking for facts
Focusing on ideas	Focusing on reality
Using mental models	Using past experience

Now simply total up the scores for column N. Do the same for column S. Whichever is your highest score describes whether your preference is for intuition or sensing. Remember that all of the Myers-Briggs personality dimensions are a sliding scale. The bigger the difference between your N and S scores, the stronger your preference for either intuition or sensing.

Understanding intuition/sensing

The intuition versus sensing dimension describes the way that you like to acquire information. Sensing individuals are grounded in facts and reality. The term 'sensing' comes from the fact that this sort of person prefers to gather facts from the five senses, looking for practical solutions based on past experience of what has or has not worked.

On the other hand, individuals with a high intuition score tend to look for patterns and associations between facts as opposed to the facts themselves. Rather than relying on the five senses, one could almost say that they use their sixth sense: intuition. They enjoy thinking about concepts and tend to leap from one idea to the next.

Table 7.4

	Intuition	Sensing
Strengths	Good at thinking up new long-term strategies Enjoy solving complex problems Good at bringing about radical change Looking for patterns and coming up with theories	Good at coming up with tactics for dealing with short-term problems Good with detail, rarely make factual errors Can be relied upon for coming up with practical solutions Often are seen as technical experts in their field
Weaknesses	Poor with detail, often ignoring them entirely Can find it difficult to express their ideas clearly to others May come up with impractical-sounding ideas or solutions Bad at following procedures	Often criticized for being insufficiently strategic Unhappy with untested ideas Dislike radical change, preferring smaller, step-by-step changes Uncomfortable when there is a lack of data to support a decision

Thinking versus feeling

To identify whether you have a preference for either thinking or feeling, complete the quick quiz. Put a tick in *either* column T or column F, depending on the statement or adjective you think describes you best.

Table 7.5

Column T	Column F
Being firm but fair	Being compassionate and understanding
Guided by logic	Guided by values
Applying reason to difficult situations	Applying empathy to difficult situations
Being critical of other people's arguments	Looking for common ground and shared values
Trying to be objective	Happy to be subjective
Respecting right and wrong	Respecting other people's choices
Thinking rationally	Thinking emotionally

Now simply total up the scores for column T. Do the same for column F. A higher T score means that your natural preference is to adopt a thinking style, while a higher F score may indicate a tendency to prefer feeling. As with the other dimensions, remember that thinking versus feeling is a sliding scale rather than a clear distinction. So it is possible to be fairly even split between both thinking and feeling.

Understanding thinking/feeling

The thinking/feeling dimension describes the way in which individuals like to make decisions. The thinking and feeling labels basically mean what you might expect.

A person who has a preference for thinking tends to look at facts and apply the rules of logic to decisions, weighing up the pros and cons before taking any course of action. A thinker often has a quite black and white view of the world and has strong views about rules and principles. A thinker often has a stance on what he or she believes to be morally or ethically right and wrong. He or she then makes decisions based on these rules.

The feeling person, on the other hand, is sensitive to other people's feelings and values and is much more concerned with the subjective impact of decisions on other people. A feeling individual seeks to understand the values and perspectives of others and tends to be far more tolerant of the lifestyle decisions that others have made, believing that all individuals are entitled to make decisions to govern their own lives.

Table 7.6

	Thinking	Feeling
Strengths	Good at weighing up different options and making decisions Able to give criticism when appropriate Seeing flaws in an argument – playing 'devil's advocate' Strong analytical skills	Good at tapping into the people-based issues and concerns of options and decisions Making efforts to attend to people's wants and needs Accepting people as they are Encouraging cooperation between different parties
Weaknesses	Can appear blunt, tactless or unconcerned with what other people think or feel May lack self-awareness, hurting other people's feelings unintentionally Can assume that other people are as competitive and driven to achieve Can be intolerant of people very different from themselves	Overly concerned with what other people might feel Dislike taking unpopular decisions Tend to shy away from criticizing others, even when it may be important to do so May be too trusting or even gullible at times

Judging versus perceiving

This is the last of the four personality dimensions. Take the test by choosing only one from each pair of statements and putting a tick in *either* column J or column P, depending on which you think describes you best.

Table 7.7

Column J		Column P
Making plans	Being spontaneous	
Liking closure	Liking options	
Enjoying stability	Enjoying flexibility	
Being organized	Being adaptable	
Disliking working under time pressure	Enjoying working under time pressure	
Making arrangements ahead of time	Avoiding planning	
Being decisive	Being open to possibilities	

If your J score is higher than your P score, you are most likely to be a judging individual. However, a higher P score means that you tend to be a perceiving individual. As with the other three dimensions, however, keep in mind that some people will sit midway between the two.

Understanding judging/perceiving

The judging/perceiving dimension describes how people deal with the external world.

People who score highly on judging like having an orderly existence; they seek closure and value decisiveness. They like making plans and using schedules to organize their time. These people can be quite single-minded and get satisfaction from completing tasks.

People who have high perceiving scores like having flexible, spontaneous lives. They enjoy keeping possibilities open; they dislike having to make decisions that could later limit their options. They enjoy moving from topic to topic, and get satisfaction from keeping multiple balls up in the air at once.

Table 7.8

	Judging	Perceiving
Strengths	Good at planning and organizing Good at making decisions quickly Taking charge in a crisis Persisting until a task is completed	Adapt well to changing circumstances Good at brainstorming and generating options Can work best under time pressure Comfortable taking risks
Weaknesses	Dislike disruptions or deviations from their plans May sometimes make decisions too quickly Dislike having pressure put on them May not be as flexible as a situation requires	May be able to make plans, but may not be so good at following them Can appear disorganized May procrastinate, putting off unpleasant tasks even though they may be important May not complete tasks that they start

GRASPING THE IMPORTANCE OF YOUR PERSONALITY

The MBTI tells us our personality preferences: we generally feel most comfortable when we behave in line with our preferences. However, the beauty of understanding these preferences is that we can choose to behave in a different way. Putting it another way, personality tells us the way that we generally prefer to behave or interact with others; it does not say anything about our abilities or lack of them. As such, **everyone has the potential to behave in a different way.**

For example, you might be a strong introvert: meaning that your natural tendency is to work alone, with the result that you can sometimes appear detached or unfriendly to approaches from other people. However, you could always make more of an effort to engage with other people, perhaps gritting your teeth and forcing yourself to turn up to team meetings and social gatherings. As another example, your MBTI type might expose a high intuition score, meaning that you might not always be as diligent with facts and figures as you might want to be. However, you could choose to make more of an effort to analyse facts and figures and double-check them carefully.

In summary, the MBTI helps you to understand how others may currently perceive you, but you can choose to change your behaviour and therefore change how they see you.

Personality and your career choices

Given that we feel most comfortable when we are allowed to behave as our preferences dictate, the MBTI may explain why you enjoy certain types of work more than others. For example, jobs that require a lot of forethought and planning tend to suit judging more than perceiving individuals. Jobs that require working in frenetic open-plan environments with a lot of discussion with colleagues and clients would tend to suit extroverts more than introverts.

Think about the four dimensions of the MBTI. What sort of work do you enjoy most, and what implications does it have for your current and future jobs?

RESPECTING PERSONALITY DIFFERENCES

The MBTI is an excellent tool for understanding personality, but it can also help us to deal with other people more effectively. We often say that we do not get on with other people because of 'interpersonal chemistry', 'personality differences', or 'a personality clash', but now that you understand a system for categorizing personality, you can analyse other people's personalities and come up with ways of interacting with them more successfully.

In Chapter 2, we talked about how to confront office politicians. However, we discussed that people are sometimes oblivious to the effects that their actions are having on others. The MBTI can give you a non-pejorative language for discussing openly differences of opinion. For example, in running a project, a judging person might like to make decisions as quickly as possible, while a perceiving person might want to keep options open for as long as possible. Consequently, the judging person might think of the perceiving individual as wasting time by refusing to allow the group to agree on a way forwards. And the perceiving individual might feel that the judging person is limited in perspective, and trying to close down a discussion too quickly without letting others contribute to the discussion. However, an understanding of the other person's MBTI type could help you to keep matters in perspective.

In order to use the MBTI model for understanding how to deal with a tricky individual, you should go through the following steps:

1. Watch the individual closely and take mental note of how he or she behaves.

2. Go through each of the MBTI dimensions and try to identify which letter best describes him or her. Match up the individual's strengths and weaknesses to each of the descriptions in this chapter. However, if you find that neither letter on each dimension describes him or her terribly well, it may be that he/she sits in the middle of each scale.

3. Seek a second opinion as to the individual's MBTI type. Explain each dimension of the MBTI to a trusted colleague and ask whether he or she agrees with your diagnosis.

4. Then try to deal with that person, playing to his/her strengths and compensating for his/her weaknesses. For example, if you are working in a team with an individual who is strongly intuitive, you may want to avoid giving them a task that involves a lot of fact-checking and detailed analysis: a task that is more suited to the 'opposite' sensing individual.

5. Finally, remember that many clashes at work may not be personal, that is, people are rarely doing something to annoy you specifically. What is often far more likely is that they are behaving in a particular way because that is the way they are. So avoid taking it personally.

GATHERING FEEDBACK FOR FURTHER INSIGHT

While personality has a huge impact on how you are perceived by others, it does not tell the entire story. It is common, for example, for people to suppress their natural personality preferences because of the working environment around them. So it might be the case that your Myers-Briggs profile does not tell the whole story of what your colleagues think of you. The only way to really find out what people think of you is to ask them. Think of it as doing market research on a product, only the product is you.

Colleagues at different levels within the organization may have different experiences, and therefore different perspectives, about you. So it is important to talk to peers and your boss, as well as people who may be more junior, such as those who report to you.

However, you obviously need to think carefully about how you are going to gather feedback on yourself, as most people's initial reaction might be to tell you what they think you would like to hear. The following step-by-step approach may help you to approach people in the most constructive fashion possible:

1. Choose half a dozen people – or 'respondents' – from whom you would value feedback. Avoid simply choosing

respondents who will tell you good things about yourself. As well as choosing people with whom you get on well, it may be worth choosing one or two individuals with whom you have clashed in the past, as they may have critical insights into how you behave when you are challenged. Friends and family are rarely the right people to choose, as they may themselves be blind to some of your weaknesses.

2. Approach each respondent to set up a meeting with him or her for only half an hour. Explain that you are making some career plans and that you would really appreciate his or her candid feedback on how you are perceived by others.

3. When it comes to the meeting itself, you need to give license to the respondent to give you a truly honest appraisal about how you come across. The biggest risk in gathering feedback is always that respondents may be reluctant to speak up about your weaknesses or fear reprisal if they do. It may even be worth writing down a rough script of what you want to say (see below for a sample script).

4. Ask about your strengths and weaknesses, and write it all down so that you can review it later. If a respondent struggles to come up with comments to make, you could prompt him or her. It may help you to ask about some of the core competencies mentioned in Chapter 4 or about particular other skills such as:

Assertiveness	Communication
Commercial awareness	Conflict handling
Data analysis	Decision-making
Influencing and persuading	Information gathering
Listening	Managing your workload
Motivation	Negotiation
Personal manner	Political awareness
Presentation skills	Relationship building
Strategic thinking	Teamwork

5. As the respondent talks, make sure that you keep your emotions in check. If you react angrily or sulkily to what he or she has to say, the respondent is unlikely to continue being honest with you, thereby defeating entirely the purpose of gathering the feedback. If you do not understand a comment, then ask for clarification; if you still do not understand, then ask for an example of when you might have behaved in that way.

6. Pay attention to what the respondent is not saying, as well as what is being said. Look for non-verbal clues that may indicate that a person is being reluctant to be too negative. If so, you may need to coax the true feelings out of one or two of your respondents.

7. Towards the end of the conversation, ask the respondent if he or she has any ideas on what you could do differently to change his or her perception of you.

8. After the respondent has finished giving you feedback, thank him or her genuinely for his/her time and candidness.

Sample script

'I know you are busy, so thank you ever so much for making the time to see me. This should only take a half hour or so of your time. I'm currently taking some time to think about my career and what I want to achieve in the next few years. As part of this career planning, I am trying to get feedback on how I come across to other people. I think I know what my strengths and weaknesses are, but you can never be certain of how you come across to other people, can you? Consequently, I'd really value it if you could give me your honest opinion of how I come across.'

Understanding the implications of your feedback

After talking to perhaps six or seven respondents, you should have amassed quite a few comments about your strengths and weaknesses. Looking at all of the comments together, you need to think about how those comments can help you. Even if you do not wholly agree with all of the comments, remember that if people have certain perceptions about you, then that is reality for them. On the one hand, you will never be able to exert perfect control over the way that others perceive you. On the other hand, if you want to develop better working relationships and succeed at work, then if, for example, one person thinks that you are arrogant, then the onus is on you to change that perception. The burden of responsibility is not on others to change. You need to make the effort.

The following questions may help you to work through the feedback:

▧ To what extent do other people's perceptions of you correspond with your own appraisal of your strengths and weaknesses? It is a good sign if the messages that other people are telling you are broadly in accordance with your own views, as this indicates a good degree of self-awareness. On the other hand, if much of the comments made about you shocked or surprised you, then you may be in danger of leading a slightly deluded existence with your colleagues, which is bound to be holding you back at work.

▧ Which of the comments worry you the most? You cannot work on everything at once, so you need to prioritize. For example, if the respondents pointed out four or five different areas of weakness, which one do you think could make the greatest difference in your career?

▧ Of the respondents, whose comments do you most value? For example, the views of your boss may have much more bearing on your career than those of a peer. This will again help you to prioritize areas for development.

▧ Looking at your weaknesses, what could you do to improve? Think about sharing your feedback with your manager or a mentor, and asking for their help in working on your areas of weakness.

▪ What are the concrete steps that you will take to improve? It may help you to jot down some notes in the form of an action plan.

Table 7.9

Difficulties	Actions	Resources	Timeframe

Draw up an action plan by jotting the four headings at the top of a sheet of paper. Then think about each column as follows:

1. **Difficulties:** what barriers or obstacles stand in the way of improving in this area?

2. **Action:** what practical steps are you going to take to bring about the change? What will you actually do to overcome each of the difficulties that you have identified? Think about the way that you like to learn or improve new skills. Do you like to read and reflect on new ideas? Or do you prefer to improve through practice, by trying out new skills and techniques?

3. **Resources:** are there training courses or books that could help you? Or are there people – either within your organization or outside it – who could help to mentor or otherwise support you? Could you benefit from observing role models who exhibit the skills or behaviours that you aspire to have? How much time and involvement would you like from them, and how will you ask them for it?

4. **Timeframe:** what is a reasonable length of time to give yourself to achieve each change? Try to set realistic deadlines for yourself. If you set out to do too much, too quickly, you may be setting yourself up for disappointment.

The more detail you can apply to the action plan, the more likely it will be that you will succeed in changing yourself and therefore other people's perceptions of you.

Over the following weeks and months, keep track of your progress against your action plan. Get further feedback from colleagues: do they see any differences in your behaviour? And if you are struggling in any areas, who could you approach for further support in refining your action plan?

8

Improving your work/life balance

Work/life balance is a phrase that is becoming increasingly popular, but there is evidence that this is a real issue as opposed to just a trendy buzz phrase. Surveys show that the length of the average working week is creeping ever higher. Both men and women say that they feel they have to spend longer at work and also experience more pressure while they are at work. Perhaps it is a symptom of increasing job insecurity in a world where a downturn in the fortunes of an employer could easily result in a wave of redundancies.

However, work need not be a treadmill that is continually accelerating. For every person who feels compelled to work harder and for longer hours to keep up with everyone else, there is another individual who is taking the decision to re-prioritize his or her personal life and work life. Balancing your work and life does not have to mean being uncommitted to your work, it simply means that you are not willing to sacrifice your home life for the sake of your work.

Some leading figures in business – often featured in the glossy magazines of Sunday papers – maintain that it is possible to 'have it all'. They argue that they can work long hours yet still have a fulfilling personal or family life. Personally, I am not convinced. Think back to the priorities exercise in Chapter 1, in which I argued that you cannot have your cake and eat it. There are only 24 hours in the day, so something has to give. But at the end of the day, this is a decision you need to make for yourself.

There are many 'downshifting' options available to you, from taking a career break or participating in a job share, to the ultimate in control over your own work and life by setting up in business for yourself.

SELF-TEST: MEASURING YOUR WORK/LIFE BALANCE

There are no objective measures of whether any particular individual is working too hard. While one individual may positively thrive on late nights and a 50-hour week, another may find even one or two late evenings at work unbearable. At the end of the day, your work/life balance is something that you must determine for yourself. So why not take this short test to determine whether your work and personal life are happily balanced?

Read the following statements and tick whether you agree or disagree with each of the following statements.

Table 8.1

	Agree	Disagree
1. I usually feel rested when I wake up in the mornings		
2. My family often complain that they do not see me enough		
3. I have at least two hobbies or leisure interests that have nothing to do with work		
4. I was happier in the past than I am now		
5. I always take my full allowance of annual leave		
6. I sometimes wake up at night worrying about problems at work		
7. I often feel that my work intrudes on my personal life		
8. If I died right now, I would be happy with the legacy I have left behind me		
9. I seldom have the energy to go out during weekday evenings		
10. I rarely have to let friends down at the last minute about social engagements		

Scoring your work/life balance

Add up your personal score as follows:

- Give yourself one point every time that you agreed with the statements numbered 2, 4, 6, 7 and 9.

- And give yourself another point each time that you disagreed with statements 1, 3, 5, 8 and 10.

Table 8.2

Your score	Comment
0–1	You have achieved a balance between your work and life that many people would envy. Two points of advice though. First, make sure that you keep your life mission in mind, in all of your future career decisions and career moves, in order to preserve this enviable balance. Second, watch out that putting your personal life above your work so much does not do harm to your future career prospects.
2–4	You seem to have a mostly satisfactory work/life balance. Work may occasionally encroach into your personal life, but your balance is still above average. But how will you preserve this balance as your career gathers pace?
5–7	It seems that your work is spilling over into your personal life. Perhaps it is more late nights or weekends at work than you would like. Or maybe the pressure of work makes you feel tired and irritable even when you are not at work. If this is not a temporary phase in your work, you may need to read the advice in this chapter and take action to address this imbalance between your work and life outside of work.
8–10	Your work seems to be the dominant force in your life. Life outside of your work hardly seems to exist. In fact, if this continues for long, you could put your health and personal relationships at risk. Can you see yourself working at this pace for the rest of your life? Read the advice in this chapter and take action soon.

But the ultimate test of your work/life balance is to ask yourself whether you are happy. So are you happy with your work and life?

EXERCISE: DEFINING YOUR PERSONAL WORK/ LIFE BALANCE

The exercises in Chapter 1 should already have helped you to define a life mission for yourself. However, if you are reading this chapter, it may be that you are still confused at to what the proper balance between your professional work and your personal or home life should be. The self-test questionnaire may have identified that there is some sort of imbalance, but this next exercise aims to make you think about the particular areas of your life that may be suffering.

In business, companies often apply what is known as a balanced scorecard to measure performance across different areas: such as profit, customer satisfaction, employee satisfaction, and new product development. The following exercise asks you to look at four more relevant areas of your life: work, relationships, personal time and growth, and physical and psychological health. Give yourself a score from 1 to 10, depending on whether you strongly disagree or agree with each statement.

1--10
Strongly disagree   Strongly agree

Table 8.3

1. Work	2. Relationships
I find myself complaining to friends and family about my job	I wish I had a partner or 'significant other' in my life
I constantly feel that I have too much to do at work	Some of my personal relationships have failed because of my work
I find it difficult to get focused while I am at work	I wish I could keep in touch with more of my friends
I wish I could spend less time with my colleagues	My sex life is not as fulfilling as it should be
I feel bored by my job	I sometimes feel lonely
3. Personal time and growth	**4. Physical and psychological health**
I don't have the time to pursue the hobbies that I enjoy	I often feel tired
I have had to give up many of the interests I used to have when I was younger	I get colds or illnesses more than most people
I feel that people (colleagues as well as friends and family) demand too much of my time and attention	I often feel under more stress than I can handle
I don't have enough time to sit and read or listen to the music that I enjoy	I wish I could get fitter or slimmer or healthier, but don't have the time or energy to do it
Other people seem to have more leisure time than me	I sometimes feel irritable or angry for no reason

Now count up your scores that you gave yourself in each area. You should now have a score for each of the four areas: each score should be between 5 and 50. The area that has the highest score is probably the one that is the least good for you at the moment.

If your highest score was in the first box, to do with work, then it seems that work/life balance is not so much of an issue for you as the fact that you no longer enjoy your work at all. Improving your work/life balance by spending fewer hours at work may provide a temporary respite, but it is not a long-term solution. You may need to go back to Chapter 1 to revisit your life mission and perhaps consult Chapter 10 on finding a new career.

On the other hand, if your highest score was in any of the other three boxes, then this chapter is filled with several popular ideas for addressing work/life imbalance. Can any of the suggestions in this chapter free up more time to invest in some of these other areas of your life?

Sanity check

This exercise was designed to make you think. Again, however, the best measure of whether your work and life truly are well balanced is your own intuition on the matter. Thinking about your own needs for a moment: are you truly happy with your work/life balance?

TAKING A CAREER BREAK

A short-term solution is to take a break from your work. Some organizations call it a leave of absence; a few other firms like to use the word sabbatical, but it all amounts to taking time away from your day-to-day work to do something completely different.

A few of the larger organizations may have formal policies about career breaks that your manager or human resources may be able to inform you about. Smaller employers are unlikely to have thought about such rules, but are likely to respond favourably if you can put a good case to your manager. Chapter 9 on negotiating might also help you to arrange a good deal.

While taking time away to recuperate and perhaps explore new facets to your life, there are a number of issues that you need to consider:

- **Money:** for many people, finding the resources to live while you are not working is the biggest issue, especially if you have a family to support, or a mortgage, car loan or other debts to pay. Many people could afford to take perhaps a month of unpaid leave, but what about six months or a year? If you are serious about taking a break from your career, you will need to spend some time poring over your finances.

- **Your employer:** many employers will hold your job for you until your return. However, you may want to spend some time thinking while you are away. How much do you really want to go back to that employer? If your work/life balance has been so poor that you need to take time away, would you be better off looking for a new job?

- **Skills:** while taking a few months away from your job might have little impact on your skills, a break of six months to a year could mean that your skills atrophy. Staying with your current employer might make it easier to step back into your old role. However, if you do have plans to change employers, would future employers be worried that you have lost touch? And how would you allay their concerns?

But what will you actually do with your time away from work? Two of the most popular options are travel and voluntary work:

- **Travel:** perhaps you want to explore new parts of the world and immerse yourself in new cultures. Alternatively, many people decide to work while they are away. The work could vary from casual farm labour to office temping work. British citizens have significant working privileges in most Commonwealth countries including Canada and Australia, while European Community members may take up work anywhere within the EC. Or if you plan to stay in one country for a year or more, you could take up a Teaching English as a Foreign Language (TEFL) course, which provides you with a formal qualification for teaching.

■ **Voluntary work:** there are many organizations that look for volunteers. Many of them offer opportunities within the UK, perhaps on landscaping projects or providing care to at-risk groups. However, there are also many organizations that operate abroad, of which the Voluntary Services Overseas (VSO) organization is perhaps the best known. It provides professionals with training and the opportunity to travel and work in often quite remote parts of the world. Most people returning from voluntary work report that, as well as gaining a new perspective on their own lives, they gain practical skills such as team working, crisis management and creative problem solving that are very attractive to employers. In considering the organization you would like to work for, make sure that you understand what financial support they are able to give you, as it varies from travelling expenses and a living allowance to nothing at all.

Other interests

While travel and voluntary work are very popular options, they are not by any means the only reasons that people choose to take a break from their work. Some people decide that they need a break simply as an extended holiday. Increasingly, many professionals feel burnt-out from the demands of their work and choose to use the break to pursue their own interests or perhaps spend time with their partner or family.

Some people can turn their noses up at people who do not use the time 'productively' in broadening their horizons or helping others. Yet you should not respond to this pressure to do something 'worthwhile'; your time and life are your own. Occasionally, it is good to be selfish – in the sense of focusing on what you really want – as opposed to worrying about what other people may think. Why should you not take time to look after your own health and well-being? If your partner and/or children are the most important part of your life, then why should you not spend time with them? Or if you want to improve your golf handicap or explore your artistic streak, then why should you not allow yourself the time to do it? After all, the cliché is true, no one on their deathbed ever says that they wish they had worked harder.

PART-TIME WORKING

Surveys show that the number of people who work part-time is growing. Traditionally, there has been a perception that part-time working is solely for those who cannot work full-time, perhaps because they are in further education or have difficulties with child-care arrangements. However, more and more people are deciding that they do not want to work full-time, freeing them up to pursue other interests and develop in areas of their life outside work.

If you are considering working part-time, you should read Chapter 9 on negotiating, which will help you to structure a case to put to your boss. However, do also make sure that you:

▪ **Work out how the work will get done.** There is no point trying to propose working part-time if you have a job that no one else can do. In many jobs, employers argue that working part-time is impossible: they might argue that clients or customers work five days a week and need access to you. So it is up to you to persuade them that it can be done. Would it be possible for you to work closely with a colleague and gradually bring his or her level of skill or expertise up to the level necessary to cover for you?

▪ **Look outside your sector.** The private sector tends to be less flexible about part-time working than the public sector. So if your current employer is reluctant to give you what you want, you may want to search other sectors for better treatment.

▪ **Know your rights.** The law dictates that part-time staff have the same employment rights as full-time staff. In practice, this means having the same benefits – such as pay, holiday, maternity pay, sick leave, pension and other benefits – on a pro rata basis.

▪ **Set clear objectives with your manager.** Traditionally, working part-time has been seen as taking a step off the route to career success. However, there should be no reason that you cannot progress within your role and organization. There is a tendency for organizations to overlook individuals who have atypical working patterns, such as working part-time or job sharing. The burden therefore falls on you to agree performance criteria with your manager for regular review, to ensure that you are not overlooked when it comes to promotions, pay rises or the other career opportunities that are available to your full-time peers at work.

JOB-SHARING

Job-sharing is a form of permanent part-time work in which two people share the responsibilities and hours, as well as the pay and benefits, of one full-time job. While the concept makes sense on an intuitive level to most people, the truth is that few organizations actively support job-sharing. Many organizations have no policies regarding job-sharing, and many managers believe that it is suitable only for relatively unimportant, perhaps administrative only, jobs within the organization. If you are serious about investigating and pursuing options for job-sharing, you may need to break new ground within your organization.

Job-sharing can take many forms. For example, the job could be split up in terms of time commitment. Each person has the same duties and responsibilities, but the individuals just work different parts of the working week. For example, one person could work the first three days of the week while the other person works for the last two days. Or one individual could work mornings while the other person covers afternoons.

Perhaps each job sharer could work a full five-day week before taking another full week off.

Alternatively, the work could be divided to play to different strengths. For example, one person might prefer to handle the administrative side of the job; the second person might prefer to spend time with clients.

Setting up a job-share

Job-sharing is a significant step, especially as there are so few good examples where it works well. Given the work involved in setting up a job-share, you need to be confident that you are fairly indispensable. If you do not have unique skills or knowledge, your organization may decide that it would be just as easy to replace you as to help you job-share. Certainly, you should read Chapter 9 to think about how best to negotiate a job-share.

Some additional points to consider before you embark on job-sharing:

▮ **The nature of your work:** some jobs are much easier to share than others. A job that requires frequent travel to meet with regular suppliers or customers could make job-sharing more difficult. How practical would it be to share your job with another person?

▮ **Career progression:** the benefits of job-sharing to the job-sharers are fairly obvious. However, sceptical managers often see job-sharers as people who want an easy life and therefore neglect them when it comes to promotions and handing out additional responsibility. How important is career progression to you? And if you still want to climb the career ladder, how could you minimize this risk?

▮ **A job-sharing partner:** how will you find a suitable partner? While a job-sharing partner would need to have similar skills and knowledge to you, you must also ensure that your personalities and methods of working are compatible.

■ **Training:** if your job-sharing partner needs to be recruited externally, how much time would be required to train your job-sharing partner?

■ **Continuity:** the key to making a job-share work is in providing continuity: a seamless service so that you do not create additional work or hassle for colleagues or customers. You will need to ensure that work does not slip through the cracks. How will information be passed from one sharer to the other? If a client calls back unexpectedly, how will you provide your job-sharing partner with all the relevant information?

■ **Contingency plans:** what could go wrong? It is in your own best interest to brainstorm potential risks and think about contingency plans if the worst happens. Just as one example, what if your job-sharing partner decides to leave the organization?

Given the scarcity of people who job-share, you may find it difficult to convince your boss. Consequently, you might want to think about networking externally (see Chapter 11) to find good examples of successful job-shares. Other job-sharers can give you advice on many of the practical issues that you might not be able to think of yourself.

OTHER FLEXIBLE OPTIONS

Career breaks and part-time working have a significant impact on your income, while job-sharing can potentially involve a lot of hard work in persuading your boss and in potential upheaval for your organization and team. Two other alternatives may allow you to work more flexibly, without requiring such dramatic changes to your income or difficulties for your colleagues. However, they are still counter-cultural in many organizations, so you would still need to invest time in preparing a case to support why you should be allowed to do it (see Chapter 9).

Annualized hours

Some organizations allow employees to log a certain number of hours over the course of a year as opposed to working 35 hours every week. So, for example, you might work 40 hours for 3 weeks, saving up 5 hours a week, which would allow you at some later stage to work only 15 hours in another week.

Having annualized hours still requires you to work a number of hours equivalent to a full-time job. So although it allows greater flexibility over the course of months or years, it does not free up any more of your time in the way that part-time working or a job share could.

In order to persuade your boss that it is a good idea, think through the following questions:

▮ How would the essential aspects of your job get done? For example, are there important team meetings at a certain time of the day that you must attend? Or what would you do if a customer demanded to speak or meet with you at short notice?

▮ Are there certain times of the month or year that would be more suitable for taking time off? You should not leave your organization in the lurch during key busy periods. For example, an accounts assistant might need to be available at the end of each month to help prepare monthly forecasts, while a retail manager might need to spend more time at work in the run-up to Christmas.

▮ What impact might it have on the other members of the team? How would you ensure that you do not unfairly pass off your duties to colleagues?

Working from home

Technology allows many of us to work from home. Parts of most office-based jobs could be done at home for perhaps one or two days of the week. Jobs that have any component of report writing, data analysis, or design – or in fact any work that requires independent thinking as opposed to frenetic brain-storming with colleagues or customers – could be done for part of the week at home.

Working from home saves you time commuting and can help you to achieve more away from the distractions of a busy work-place. Some organizations already encourage employees in certain functions to work from home – you may hear the term 'location independent worker' bandied about – as it helps them to cut down on office overheads. However, some employers are sceptical of the benefits and worry that employees at home could be using the time to slack off.

In selling the idea to your manager, you may need to think about:

- What technology – such as computer equipment, additional telephone lines, fax machines and so on – would you require your organization to provide you with? And what would you personally be willing to pay for?

- How many days a week would you want to work from home? Remember that being physically present in the office is a good way to keep up with the grapevine and prevent colleagues from manoeuvring politically against you while you are away from the office. Showing your face also serves to remind colleagues that you exist, otherwise you could risk being passed over for interesting work opportunities and promotions.

- How would your work output be measured? How would you be able to convince your manager that you were doing some-thing useful at work as opposed to taking extended lie-ins?

GOING SOLO

Deciding to work for yourself is the ultimate form of control over your work and life. You are the boss, deciding where and when you will work. However, working from home does not suit everyone. Before we discuss how to make it happen, you might want to complete the following questionnaire to see whether it would suit you or not.

SELF-TEST: MEASURING YOUR WORK DISCIPLINE

Tick whether you 'agree' or 'disagree' with each of the following statements about your attitudes and beliefs about working for yourself.

Table 8.4

	Agree	Disagree
1. I enjoy actively networking with customers or clients		
2. I like to work on one project or task at a time		
3. I am happy to take financial risks		
4. I value having job security		
5. I don't mind blurring the distinction between work and home life		
6. I like having my weekends completely free from work		
7. I am good at ignoring distractions and motivating myself to work		
8. I enjoy the buzz of working with colleagues		
9. I am good at budgeting and dealing with finances		
10. I do not like to talk about myself		
11. I could put up with having irregular pay from month to month		
12. I like having paid holidays at particular times of the year		

Understanding your work discipline

Calculate your organization's score as follows:

▨ Award yourself 1 point every time you ticked 'agree' for all of the odd-numbered statements, 1, 3, 5, 7, 9 and 11.

▨ Also give yourself another point if you disagreed with the even-numbered statements 2, 4, 6, 8, 10 and 12.

Table 8.5

Your score	Comment
0–4	Your score indicates that your natural tendencies are more suited to being an employee rather than a self-employee. The reality is that most people who are self-employed actually work longer and more irregular hours than those who are employees. In addition, self-employees generally have less job and pay security than employees. Given that you seem to value financial security and having a regular salary, evenings and weekends to yourself, and holidays, your best bet may be to stay in employment. Would any of the other options within this chapter be better suited to you for improving your work/life balance?
5–8	Your score sits midway between those suited to remaining in employment and those who are definitely suited to setting up in business on their own. A simple questionnaire like this is unable to tell you what you should do with your life: perhaps you should read the remainder of this chapter to help you think about whether you would really want to work for yourself or not.
9–12	You may have the attitude that you need to work for yourself. You seem to be happy to promote and market yourself. And you have a realistic view of the potentially longer hours and financial risks that typically go with working for yourself. The problem with working for yourself is that you do not get paid when you are not working, making self-employment actually harder work for many people. You may end up working longer hours, but you would have more control over your work and life. For the most part, you would get to choose when you work.

Setting up on your own

Statistics from the Department of Trade and Industry show that a large proportion of new businesses go bust within their first year. To ensure that you do not fall into this category, you should ask yourself the following questions:

▪ **What service or products would you offer?** What particular skills are you able to offer that could make you stand out from potential competitors? Marketing experts speak of developing a niche market for yourself. If you do not have something unique – perhaps in terms of quality or value for money – then why would anyone want to buy from you?

▪ **Who would your customers or clients be?** Do you have a strong network of potential customers or clients? If not, how would you get one? Look into joining professional networks, such as through your local Business Link or Chamber of Commerce. Also, there is a big difference between having supportive contacts saying that they would buy from you and having firm commitments or even binding contracts. Make sure that you can distinguish between real customers and people who make only empty promises.

▪ **How would you finance your venture?** Apart from the physical start-up costs of having to buy equipment, rent premises or even hire employees, do not forget that you might have no income for a few months until customers' cash starts to come in. Apart from your own savings, look also into the wide variety of sources of funding that could be available, such as high street banks, finance houses, venture capital trusts, government grants, and private investors such as friends or family.

▪ **How would you deal with cash flow problems?** Research by both the government and high street banks indicates that many small businesses fail because of poor cash flow. There can be a gap of many months between you delivering your products or services to a customer and having them pay up: a gap during which your business is out of pocket. Learn the difference between cash and profit, and seek advice on how to manage it.

▪ **What are your contingency plans?** There will always be problems and setbacks. A potential customer who gives you verbal agreement to place a large order could change their mind at the last moment, leaving you in the lurch. A supplier could go into liquidation. You could fall ill. Take time to brainstorm a list of potential problems: no matter how unlikely they might seem at this moment in time. How would you cope with each and every one of these problems?

Having pointed out all of these obstacles, however, there are many people who do set up in business for themselves and enjoy it hugely. It all comes down to risk versus reward. The risks of setting up on your own are far greater than working for someone else as an employee. However, the rewards are also potentially greater: not just financially, but also in terms of the ability to take complete control of your working life.

9

Negotiating for more

We all work for a variety of reasons. The simple truth is that many of us work because we need to earn a living. Most of us are unlikely to turn down a pay rise if it were to be offered to us! On the other hand, I have already mentioned that money is not the sole motivator for everyone. We want to do work that keeps us interested. And we want to do work that allows us to have a life outside of our jobs as well. We all want more.

At the end of the day, we all *want* more money, more interesting or challenging work, and the best work/life balance possible: or some combination of these. But these can crop up in different ways. For example, having read the other chapters within this book, you may decide that you want to:

■ Ask for a better pay package from your current employer to reflect the contribution that you make at work.

■ Get a better work/life balance by asking to work part-time, in a job-share, or perhaps from home for a few days every week.

- Change the nature of your work, perhaps by altering your job description, changing your reporting line, or getting a secondment to another department.
- Put a proposal to your employer for financial support and time off to do a lengthy training course.
- Resign from your job but continue to work for the department on a freelance or consultancy basis.
- Agree with a prospective employer the best possible job role, salary and reward package possible – as well as bargaining over your starting date – before signing on the dotted line.

The list could go on and on. We all *want* so many things. And this chapter shows you how you might be able to get them.

STRIKING THE RIGHT BALANCE

Before we talk about *how* to negotiate, it is worth thinking about *what* to negotiate for. What do you really want out of your life and career? If you completed the exercises in Chapter 1, you should have a life mission statement that you can refer back to. Use this as a 'sanity check' before deciding what you want to negotiate.

It is easy to get fixated on money, on salaries and the size of our bonuses. Unfortunately, many people in our society tend to equate salary with social worth. But is money what you really want to make you satisfied with your work and happy in your life? Is it really money that you want, or are you looking to meet other aspirations: for more responsibility, a greater variety of work, less stress in your work, new challenges? There is a big difference between financial success and career satisfaction.

So think carefully before you decide to negotiate a bigger and better package. Is more money what you really want, or would a change in your job role or career direction actually be more fulfilling? You have been warned.

SELF-TEST: EVALUATING YOUR NEGOTIATING EFFECTIVENESS

Negotiation is a particular skill that few of us are good at. Many of us feel uncomfortable asking for what we want out of life, with the result that we simply do not get it!

Read the following statements and tick whether you agree or disagree with each of the following statements when approaching a negotiation.

Table 9.1

	Agree	Disagree
1. I set clear objectives before entering into a negotiation		
2. I prepare arguments to support my case		
3. I see negotiation as a situation where there can only be one winner		
4. I make a list of points that I would be willing to concede on		
5. I occasionally lose my temper when negotiations do not go my way		
6. I know that I tend to give in too easily		
7. I think that negotiations should be handled in one sitting		
8. I think about the difference between what I want and what I need		
9. I think about the point at which I would walk away from a negotiation rather than settle for an unsatisfactory deal		
10. I am prepared to issue an ultimatum if I do not get what I want		

Scoring your negotiating effectiveness

Calculate your personal score as follows:

- Give yourself one point every time that you agreed with the statements numbered 1, 2, 4, 8 and 9.

- And add another point disagreeing with statements 3, 5, 6, 7 and 10.

Table 9.2

Your score	Comment
0–3	You seem to have a fairly naïve view of negotiation. Good negotiation is all about the preparatory work: establishing clearly in your own mind what you would ideally like versus what you would be prepared to accept as a minimum. The next time that you approach a salary negotiation or try to persuade a boss or colleague that you want to change anything about your work, this chapter could prove invaluable in maximizing your chances of success.
4–7	You have an average understanding of negotiation. Perhaps you try to plan before negotiations, but do not succeed in sticking to your plan. Or perhaps you do not know exactly how to prepare. In either case, this chapter should help you to improve your negotiation effectiveness.
8–10	You have a good appreciation of the preparation that is needed before any negotiation. However, we can all improve: so is there anything from this chapter that would help you to negotiate even more effectively?

STEP-BY-STEP NEGOTIATION

When we use the word 'negotiate', it tends to be associated with hostile situations. We tend to think about negotiation as a process of psychological warfare: of two hostile parties sticking rigidly to their positions, trying to push their cause or side of the argument, and trying at all costs to avoid 'losing face' by giving in. However, it is far more helpful to think of negotiation as a process whereby you plan to trade off some of your more superficial wants to ensure that you get what you *need* for your career. In particular, be prepared to balance short-term, tactical career benefits against longer-term, strategic gains.

At work, we most commonly want to negotiate over money, changes to the nature of our work, or our job roles. The following steps should help you to cover all of the important points to maximize your chances of getting what you want.

Step 1: determining your objectives

It may sound obvious that you need to set a clear objective before you enter into any negotiation. Think about what you would like to achieve out of the negotiation. I would actually recommend that you write this down as a way of making your objective as clear and concrete as possible. The risk of not having a clear objective is that you could end up cutting off your nose to spite your face. For example, a prospective employer who thinks that you are making unreasonable demands could end up retracting their offer and leaving you with nothing.

After establishing a clear objective, think also about the following four areas:

- What would you ideally **want** to get out of the negotiation? Create a wish list of all of the elements of a deal that you would like if at all possible. You are unlikely to get all of them, but it will help you to make trade-offs later on.

- What do you actually **need**? What would you be willing to accept as a minimum? For example, you might want to be offered a £50,000 salary but have in the back of your mind that you would only need to be offered £45,000 to take the job. In particular, think about:
  - What concessions would you be willing to make?
  - What is your absolute bottom line and at what point would you decide to walk away?

- How are you going to **justify** what you are asking for? Why should the other party give you what you want? Think about reasons to support your case. Try to include in your argument benefits that the other person would gain, or perhaps risks that they would avoid, such as:
  - your improved motivation;
  - greater work productivity;
  - staff retention (of you);
  - retention of knowledge and expertise;
  - and so on.

▓ What **counterarguments** is the other person likely to raise, and what would your counter-counterarguments be to each of those?

Also keep in mind the short-term, tactical versus long-term, strategic element of what you are negotiating for. For example, consider that you are offered two jobs. One employer might offer you a fantastic reward package while the other might offer a more modest package, but the second employer might have a better brand and reputation. The first employer might offer a better tactical gain, but it might be the second that will offer greater career opportunities in the longer term.

In thinking through such issues, it may help you to take advice from friends or colleagues whom you can trust in preparing for a negotiation. In addition, if you are preparing to negotiate a deal with a potential employer that approached you through a headhunter or recruitment firm, you should also seek their advice in order to get a good deal.

Step 2: presenting your case

Think about how you will introduce the topic that you want to negotiate about. It may come as a surprise to your (prospective) manager or colleague, so think about the best time and place to bring up the subject. Would it be best to wait until your appraisal or regular monthly meeting, or do you need to discuss it more urgently than that?

In addition, if you are presenting a complex argument, what written documentation might you want to prepare? For example, in negotiating with a prospective employer, you might write a short note of the details of your pay request. If you were proposing a job-share, perhaps you could print off examples of successful job-shares from the Internet. If you were trying to argue for financial support for a training course, you might want to get the brochures or marketing literature.

Having thought of the *content* of what you will say, however, you should not forget the *manner* in which you approach the other party. What sort of tone should you adopt? Clever use of your interpersonal skills could help the other party to be more positively predisposed to your requests.

Step 3: identifying the other person's position

When you have broached the subject and presented your case, try not to force the discussion. You should hopefully have spent time and energy on thinking about the best way to argue your case; on the other hand, if your request is at all unusual or unexpected, the other party is likely to need some time to formulate a proper response. If he or she asks for some time to think about it, you should let him/her do so.

The other party might have some concerns or questions for you. Consequently, you should spend some time determining the other person's stance:

- **What concerns or objections does he or she have?** Embedded in these objections are likely to be a set of needs that he/she feels must be met before giving in to your demands. For example, a manager might need to be convinced that the quality of your work or the productivity of the team would not suffer.

- What **further information** does he or she require to help make up his/her mind?

Even if some of the other person's demands or expectations seem unreasonable, you should be respectful of his or her opinion. You could try phrases such as 'I can understand that you are worried that …' or 'I can see why you are reluctant to …'

You may be able to answer some of their objections immediately. 'I can understand that you don't want to do X, but what if I could show you that …' On the other hand, if you cannot think of a suitable response straightaway, do not be afraid to call a halt to the meeting in order to allow you time to do more research before setting up a second meeting.

Step 4: agreeing compromises

A negotiation should not be a battle between two sides, even though both you and the other party might be feeling quite strongly about your respective positions by now. Therefore the next step is to think back to your list of wants and needs and prepare to make concessions. Be prepared to give in on some of your wants or tactical gains in order to ensure that you get what you need, such as any longer-term, strategic gains. If at all possible, though, the trick here is to offer conditional concessions ('I'll do this, if you do that') as opposed to one-sided concessions ('I'll do this for you'). In addition, keep emphasizing how your proposals would also meet the other person's needs. Here are some examples of the sorts of tactics you could be employing:

▓ 'If I were to accept the lower salary, would you agree to give me a £3,000 pay rise in four months' time? That meets your need to keep the opening salary lower, doesn't it?'

▓ 'What if I were to spend two months training someone to take over on the help desk? Would that be enough to persuade you that I wouldn't be letting the team down and for you to let me take this secondment?'

▓ 'If you see your way to letting me work from home for half of the week, perhaps I could forgo part of my car allowance. What if I gave up, say, 60 per cent of my car allowance?'

▓ 'I understand that you're worried that I'd just use the company to sponsor my course and then leave the company. But what if the company provided half of the course fees as an interest free loan instead of giving it to me in cash?'

Successful negotiations involve some discussion back and forwards, making suggestions and agreeing trade-offs along the way. Some people get embarrassed at the prospect of bargaining over money, but there is no need to be, as long as you prepare carefully and keep the discussion professional at all times.

Be patient and be prepared to make concessions gracefully, but keep your objective in mind to ensure that you do not accept a worse deal than you had planned. Keep your strategic career goals in mind. For example, if you want to negotiate working for four days a week, keep in mind the reasons you want to work part-time. Is it because you are entirely happy with your job but want more time to concentrate on endeavours that interest you, or is it because you actually do not like your job but want some time off to think about what else you would rather be doing? These two very different reasons would imply perhaps different negotiation strategies, as you might be able to get away with being more aggressive in the second case if you really could not care less about the job.

Step 5: sealing the deal

When you believe that you have reached an agreement that satisfactorily meets the needs of both yourself and the other party, it is worth spending a few minutes summarizing what has happened. This will help you to ensure that there has been no misunderstanding.

However, there might be occasions when you are unable to reach a mutually satisfactory deal. If so, make sure that you end the discussion professionally, keeping your temper or any true feelings in check. This would allow you, for example, to leave the matter for six months and attempt another round of negotiation then.

Finally, if you have reached a deal, this is the stage at which the paperwork and any legalities need to be handled. If it is a reward package that you are negotiating over, you should ask (politely) when you can expect a written contract. Or if you are agreeing to change your job role in some way, you should lay out a timetable of the key steps to ensure that the matter does not get put off repeatedly.

UNDERSTANDING YOUR WORTH

The most common form of negotiation in the workplace takes place over pay and benefits. We should all negotiate when we are considering taking a job with a new company. And we should all negotiate whenever our role changes substantially: either because of promotion, transfer or changes that we initiate.

   However, before you know what you can ask for, you need to determine what you are worth. It is in your best interests to do some research to benchmark what you could be earning:

■ **Look at job advertisements.** What kind of salary are other employers offering for a similar role?

■ **Look at the whole package and not only the cash element.** Calculate the benefits and bonus elements too. Medical insurance, use of a mobile phone or a car, gym membership, all of these could enhance your quality of life.

■ **Talk to recruitment consultants** who specialize in your field of expertise. However, do take their advice with a pinch of salt, as they make a living out of putting people into jobs. Unscrupulous recruitment consultants could put you into the wrong job to make their commission.

■ **Look at salary surveys.** There are many of these on job Web sites which provide information collected from dozens of other employers.

However, be careful that you look at the right comparison groups when researching what you think you should be paid. Salary is influenced by a number of factors other than your performance:

■ **Supply and demand.** Employers are willing to pay a premium to attract candidates of the right calibre in areas where there is a shortage of skills. In recent years, for example, this has favoured employees with certain IT and strategic planning skills.

- **Location.** For example, a job in a large city might attract a premium over a similar job in a smaller town.
- **Company performance.** A healthy and growing company may be able to pay much more than a company that is losing customers, making redundancies or seeing a decline in its share price. If you are working in a company that is not performing particularly well, be careful before you demand the same salary as someone in a similar role in a company that is performing well. Your boss might ask you, 'Well, why don't you get a job there then?'

Warning: is money what you really want?

I mentioned it at the start of the chapter and I will mention it again. In my coaching work, I often find that people initially think that more money will make them feel happier. But on investigating further, I often find that they want more money because they see it as compensation for having to put up with something unsatisfactory in their work. Don't let this happen to you.

Changing career track

Surveys over the last 40 years have shown that people are becoming increasingly mobile in their careers. It is not unusual for people to move from employer to employer every three to four years. In some fast-moving industries such as investment banking or IT, it is not uncommon to change jobs every two years. In addition, many recruitment consultants advise that a change of role or employer is important every five or so years to ensure that you remain employable.

Job changes are sometimes prompted by factors outside of our control: redundancy, being fired, illness, or the needs of our families. But there are occasions when we may want to make the switch to a new employer. The exercises in Chapter 1 may already have helped you to identify that a change is needed in your working life. Too many people put up with being unhappy in their work; they believe that it is acceptable because it pays the bills and 'it could be worse'. But think of how much better it could be. Being motivated – or even passionate – about your work could help you to succeed so much more.

However, it is important to distinguish between dissatisfaction because of your work versus unhappiness with your work*place*. Are your reasons for unhappiness down to your current working environment, the culture and your colleagues? Or are you unhappy because you do not enjoy the nature and type of work that you do?

This chapter aims to answer these questions. And, if you do decide that drastic action is required, what options are there for retraining to do an entirely different job?

EXERCISE: SEARCHING FOR REASONS TO LIKE WORK

It is human nature to be dissatisfied with what we have. We always want what we do not have. When it comes to looking for a new employer or a new job, it can be easy to believe that the grass is greener on the other side of the fence. This next exercise is designed to help you take a measured perspective of your current working situation.

On a blank sheet of paper, copy out the two headings and write down at least 10 reasons why you most like your work, colleagues, company and culture. Only when you have come up with 10 good points should you allow yourself to work on 10 reasons why you dislike your work.

Table 10.1

Likes	Dislikes

You may want to refer back to this table of likes and dislikes as you complete the questionnaires and other exercises in this chapter.

SELF-TEST: MEASURING YOUR WORK DISSATISFACTION LEVELS

This next questionnaire has two aims. First, it can help you to figure out how dissatisfied (or satisfied) you are with your current job. Second, it can help to point out possible reasons you are unhappy with your work.

Read the following statements and tick as to whether you agree or disagree with each of the statements. Do not spend too much time thinking about any individual statement. Go through the statements fairly quickly and select the first answer that comes into your head.

Table 10.2

Question	Agree
1. I often feel that I do not fit in at work	
2. I don't get to use my strongest skills in the job that I am doing	
3. I don't like the way that decisions are made at work	
4. If I am honest, I don't think that I am as good at this job as most of the people in my team	
5. I do not like the way that I am typically treated by other people at work	
6. I wish I could be doing a completely different job	
7. The things that other people at work regard as important just do not seem important to me	
8. I entered into my profession because members of my family are in this line of work	
9. I have little or no respect for my boss	
10. I have reached a plateau in my work: there are few challenges left	
11. I don't like to socialize with people from work too often: I spend enough time with them during the day	
12. I am not interested in keeping up to date with developments in my field	
13. I do not feel that I am in control of my own work	
14. I struggle to cope with some of the aspects of my work	

Looking at your overall work dissatisfaction

Let us look at the first aim of this questionnaire, which was to help you think about how unhappy you are with your work in general.

To calculate your dissatisfaction score, give yourself one point for every statement that you agreed with.

Table 10.3

Your score	
0–5	Congratulations. You seem to be very happy in your work. You seem to get intrinsic satisfaction from the nature of the work itself. And you seem to enjoy working with your colleagues as well.
6–10	You probably fall into the same category as most people in the working population. You enjoy parts of your work and get on with some of the people that you work with: but there are elements of your job and some colleagues that annoy or bore you. Ignoring the results of this quiz for a moment, would you say that you would be happy to stay in your current role in this company for the next five years? If not, perhaps you need to read the rest of this chapter to investigate possible changes.
11–14	You seem to be very unhappy about your work. Perhaps you have lost interest in the day-to-day nature of the work itself. Or perhaps the problem lies with the company culture or some of the colleagues around you or even your boss. Being very unhappy at work over long periods of time can have negative effects on both your psychological and physical health. So how much of this are you willing to put up with? What keeps you at your job?

Understanding why you may be dissatisfied

Now let us look at the second aim of the test: helping you to identify the aspects of your work that you are most unhappy with. In very broad terms, people tend to be unhappy with either the way that people behave and treat each other at work (company culture dissatisfaction) or the nature of the work itself (intrinsic work dissatisfaction).

Count up your scores on these two dimensions as follows:

- Give yourself one point on the company culture dissatisfaction scale if you agreed with the odd numbered statements 1, 3, 5, 7, 9, 11 and 13.

- Give yourself one point on the intrinsic work dissatisfaction scale if you agreed with the even numbered statements 2, 4, 6, 8, 10, 12 and 14.

Table 10.4

Write your **company culture** **dissatisfaction** score here	Write your **intrinsic work dissatisfaction** score here

Read what these may mean for you and your career as follows:

Company culture dissatisfaction

If you have a high score (between five to seven points) on this scale, then it might be that you do not like the culture of your organization and/or your colleagues. The simplest definition of culture is 'the way we do things around here'. So it is not about the physical working environment, but the way that people make decisions, behave and treat each other on a day-to-day basis. The culture in one company, for instance, might give employees a lot of autonomy to make decisions, while another might require employees to submit decisions to extensive scrutiny from managers within the company. Neither is right or wrong, but one may fit your preferences more than the other.

Company culture also tends to be reflected in the policies, processes and procedures that govern employee behaviour. For example, the bonus system in one company could reward competition and individual success, while in another company it could reward collaboration and team results. Again, neither is better or worse, but one may suit your style of working more than the other.

Options to consider, if your current company culture seems to be the issue, include:

1. **Do nothing.** Think back to other companies that you may have worked in and compare the company culture there with the one that you are in now: how bad is the situation that you are currently in? Is it a long-term problem or are you perhaps merely experiencing a temporary bad patch: perhaps some disagreements with colleagues at work? Think about how you felt when you first joined the company: were things better then?

2. **Try to get a transfer to another team.** If you work in a large enough company, you might be able to seek a transfer to another department or business unit. For example, many companies run their business units with their own IT, finance, HR and administration departments. In large companies, there may be a few cultural similarities between business units, but there are also likely to be many differences. Could you find another business unit to take you on?

3. **Tackle the local culture.** If the problems are limited to just a few of your colleagues, is there anything that you could do to tackle them directly? If political manoeuvring is at play, remember that Chapter 2 contains advice on handling office politics.

4. **Look for a new employer.** If you believe that the problems cannot be solved in any other way, you may decide to look for a new employer. However, you must be clear about how you will identify the right sort of company culture for you. How would you describe those cultural characteristics, and, more importantly, how would you go about investigating whether potential employers could provide you with the right culture?

5. **Talk to headhunters and recruitment consultants.** Approach the recruitment companies that work in your field of expertise and find out about the sorts of cultures elsewhere. However, be aware that many of these companies work on a commission basis for successfully placing candidates. So be careful not to let an over-zealous recruiter force you to accept a job in a company that does not meet all of your cultural criteria.

Intrinsic work dissatisfaction

If you have a high score (again, between five and seven points) on this dimension, then it may be that you do not – or used to, but no longer – enjoy the nature of your work. Perhaps you do not feel that you are able to exercise your strongest skills, or the ones that you most enjoy using at work. Or perhaps you have been in the job for so long that there is no challenge any more.

If you no longer enjoy the actual work itself, then leaving the company and taking a similar job in a different company may not provide the answer, as the work would probably be broadly similar. You have four general options for improving your satisfaction with the intrinsic nature of your work:

1. **Talk to your manager.** The first thing to do is to take the time to analyse which parts of your job you least enjoy. Then think about how you would ideally like to change what you do on a day-to-day basis to make you happier. Once you have put some thought into the matter, go talk to your manager and explain the situation, that perhaps you feel jaded by your work and want to shift your role.

2. **Talk to your organization.** If your manager is not particularly helpful, do not give up immediately. If you decide that you like the culture and the other perks of working for the company, you should next try to find any other opportunities within the company before quitting. If your current manager is not keen to let you try out a new role, are there

other managers who might give you that chance? Moving to a new job within a different department within an existing employer is less risky than leaving the company entirely. Many larger businesses advertise jobs internally: are there other roles that you might be interested in? Alternatively, try expanding your network (see Chapter 11) within the company to approach other managers directly. Look for jobs that allow you to use some of the skills that you already have as well as requiring you to learn new ones.

3. **Do nothing.** You could continue in the same job role with your current employer and continue to be unhappy with the work. But perhaps you decide that you enjoy the company of the rest of the team or that the pay package is good enough to put up with it for a while, and perhaps you do not want to 'rock the boat' because the job provides you with financial security and allows you to focus your energies on your life outside work. On the other hand, is this an option that you would be prepared to put up with for the rest of your life?

4. **Think about a new line of work.** It may be time for a complete career change. Just because you have worked and/or qualified in one role does not mean that you must continue doing the same work for the rest of your life. Do the aspirations identified in the eulogy exercise in Chapter 1 point you in any new directions?

Sanity check

Before we move on, it is worth doing a 'sanity check' on the results. Looking at your scores on the questionnaire as well as what you wrote down as your likes and dislikes in the first exercise in this chapter, do you agree with the diagnosis or not? The questionnaire is designed to help you understand how you feel about work. But you should not let a simple questionnaire like this alone decide whether you should set off in a new career direction or not. What does your gut instinct and intuition tell you? How do you feel about the result of the test?

EXERCISE: CHOOSING THE RIGHT COMPANY CULTURE

There is no 'best' or ideal company culture. What suits one person may be completely at odds with the preferences of another person. If you have identified that you enjoy the nature of your work, but want to move to another company with a culture that more suits your style of working, then this exercise may help you to select the right company for you.

There are many different dimensions to company culture. Take your time to think through the following areas:

- **How important is sociability to you?** There are some companies that encourage employees to socialize or 'bond' together. For example, many large firms send trainees on induction programmes at corporate universities (lasting weeks or months), that are as much about social networking as training for the job. Once on the job, some companies actively promote socializing within teams. Other companies make far less effort to do so, with the result that employees tend to keep a greater distance between their personal and work life. Which end of the scale would you prefer?

- What level of **autonomy** do you enjoy in your work? Do you like to have considerable input into what you should be working on and how you should be doing it? Or would you prefer to let others make some of the tougher decisions for you, and instead provide you with more explicit instructions on how tasks should be done? You could also think about it another way, in terms of how much contact you would wish to have with your manager. Would you prefer to have a manager who leaves you alone, or would you rather have more frequent meetings with your manager so that you can discuss your progress and any problems?

- To what extent do you like to follow **processes and procedures**? Do you like to have clear policies and guidelines that lay out the company's accepted methods of doing tasks? Or do you prefer to be measured on outcomes and results: to have much more freedom to try new solutions to problems? Another way of thinking about this dimension is to consider the extent to which you feel comfortable taking risks. Having established processes and procedures tends to reduce the freedom to take decisions, but also minimizes the risk of doing something wrong. Conversely, having fewer processes and procedures may allow much more decision-making freedom, but with a greater possibility of making a mistake.

▓ What are your needs for **communication**? Do you like to spend a lot of time in face-to-face meetings with your boss, team members, colleagues and customers, or do you prefer to receive communication through e-mail, newsletters and corporate intranets?

▓ How important are **teamwork and collaboration** to you? Do you like to work in an environment that supports cooper-ation and group effort along with team targets? Or are you happier working more independently, perhaps in a more competitive environment that rewards individual success?

There are no right or wrong answers, as the culture that suits you may not suit someone else. What one person describes as well-ordered, another could describe as bureaucratic. As with some of the other exercises in this book, make sure that you are thinking about what would make you happy, not what your friends, family or work acquaintances might deem acceptable. It may help you to write down a few notes as to how you would describe the ideal company culture: what would it *feel* like to work there?

Eventually, when you are satisfied that you have decided on the sort of company that you would like to work for, keep this in mind when you meet prospective employers. Chapter 12 also has further advice for evaluating prospective employers.

CAREER OPTIONS

Before you think about a drastic career change, consider some of the less radical ways of changing the way that you work. Chapter 8 presented ideas on how to adapt your existing role to fit your work/life balance needs and long-term career aspirations. But there are other ways in which to work that sit somewhere in between being a permanent, full-time employee and a completely independent self-employee. Which of these could work for you?

- **Becoming an interim manager.** Companies sometimes find themselves facing a short-term issue that they do not have the resource to cope with. In such situations, they may look to bring in an interim manager, a seasoned individual with experience and a track record of success in dealing with similar issues to those they are facing. Interim managers are typically matched up with potential employers through specialist recruitment firms or interim management associations. The pay can be very good, but this is usually matched by an expectation that you will work hard to deliver on a project against quite tough deadlines.

- **Choosing a portfolio career.** This involves moving towards holding two or more different part-time jobs. For example, you might work for a few days a week with your current employer while working a few more days a week for another organization that you have a particular interest in, and perhaps doing some voluntary work for a few days every month. By combining different jobs, it may be possible to meet different personal needs. As just one example, if your current job bores you but pays well, you might decide to continue working there on a part-time basis for the financial security, allowing you to seek more interesting work for the rest of the time.

- **Working as a non-executive director.** Again, this is realistically only an option for more experienced managers who have had involvement in running companies. Non-executives typically spend time working with the senior managers of a company for a few days every month, providing an external perspective to issues and plans that are currently being discussed within the company. If you have some valuable experience, there are many smaller companies as well as not-for-profit organizations that need the sound judgement and contribution to decision-making that an experienced manager can bring.

▧ **Moving into consultancy.** Many roles that are done on behalf of an employer can also be provided by external consultants. Not all consultants call themselves consultants, but what they have in common is that they make a living out of providing their specialist expertise, advice and support to clients on a fee basis. The range of consultants is very broad: from marketing consultants to HR, strategy and IT consultants, PR and recruitment agencies, to financial advisors and professional trainers. Consulting tends to bring more variety than working 'in-house'; it could involve working with a new client every couple of months, or maybe working with multiple clients at the same time. However, consulting work is wholly dependent on finding new clients so you might find yourself getting involved in business development activity such as networking, meeting and pitching to clients for business, writing proposals and negotiating contracts.

If any of these options appeal, then I would suggest taking two steps to find out more about them. First, use desk research tools – library journals, the Internet, books – to find out more about these roles. Second, use your networking skills (Chapter 11) to find people who are already doing what you are thinking about doing.

MAKING A DRASTIC CAREER CHANGE

If you have tried other ways of changing the nature of your work but are still feeling frustrated, then now may be the time to consider a complete change of career. Look back at Chapter 1. Do any of the exercises there – especially the values quiz and the ARC table – push you in the direction of any particular careers? What do you feel passionate about in your life? If you have any interests that truly excite you, would it be possible to make a living – or at least part of a living – out of those? If you are unable to come up with ideas yourself, perhaps you could ask friends what they think might be a good career choice for you.

Once you have identified possible future careers, ask yourself the following questions. Again, it is worth writing down your initial thoughts. Then, when you come to doing more rigorous research, you can compare your findings with your initial ideas and preconceptions about the job.

- What attracts you to that career choice?
- What skills would this job allow you to exercise?
- How much do you actually know about the day-to-day work involved in that career?
- Why do you think you might enjoy it?

However, do also think about possible downsides or constraints:

- What retraining would be necessary to do this job?
- How would you fund any retraining?
- How easy would it be to get a job once trained in this field?
- No job is perfect. So what would the negatives be of doing this job for the rest of your life?
- How would this career change affect your partner or any dependants?

At this stage, it is worth keeping options open. The risk is that you could settle for one career choice too early, eliminating other possible choices that could actually be a better fit for your skills, interests and aspirations. Ideally, you should proceed to the next stage – researching your new career – with at least a handful of different options.

RESEARCHING YOUR NEW CAREER

Embarking on a new career path needs serious consideration. It takes time and effort and often a lot of money as well. So you need to gather as much information as possible to ensure that any potential new career will definitely make you happier in your working life:

1. Use the Internet and library resources to read up on the field.
2. Contact the trade body or association of your chosen profession (if there are any); some professions also have their own trade union. For example, acupuncturists typically do courses that are approved by the British Acupuncture Council. Vets need to get in touch with the British Veterinary Association, while veterinary nurses should consider contacting the British Veterinary Nursing Association. However, do be aware that some professions are governed by several bodies. Get each trade organization to send you as much information as possible. Also ask if they have a list of people that you could approach to meet and talk to.
3. Contact the recognized colleges, universities or other organizations that can provide the training in this field. Find out about the course (see the section on 'continuing professional and personal development' in Chapter 4 for more questions to ask). Also, ask to see if you could talk to ex-students about the course and what they did after they qualified.
4. Use your own network (see Chapter 11) to find people already in that profession to talk to. Also, try to talk to customers of that profession. For example, if you are

thinking about becoming a personal financial adviser, then try to find some people who have had financial advice. Ask them about their experience of coming into contact with that profession, what was good and bad?

5. Read the jobs press to look out for careers events. These might provide a one-stop shop opportunity for you to meet people within the industry and gather information on employers, training, and finance for training.

Desk research – such as using the Internet or library resources – can only get you so far. The most valuable information comes from the people that you meet. When you do find people to speak to, good topics to ask about might include:

- The work itself:
  - What do they do on a day-to-day, hour-by-hour basis? How do they spend their time?
  - What do they most enjoy about their work?
  - What are the worst or most boring aspects of the job?
  - What are the hours and working patterns like?

- The industry:
  - What kind of employment opportunities are there in this area? Do people tend to set up in business on their own and work for themselves? Are there franchise opportunities that will provide you with marketing support for a fee, or is it possible to join a small, medium or larger-sized employer to work with people in the same profession?
  - Who are the customers or clients for this profession? And how do you find them?
  - Is the profession growing? What social and economic trends are influencing the growth or stability of the industry?

- The training:
  - Have they always worked in this field? If not, what did they do before? And why did they change careers?

- What was their experience of switching careers? What pitfalls did they encounter? And what advice would they have for you?
- What do they know about the different training courses and routes to accreditation or recognition within the profession?

EXERCISE: GAP ANALYSIS AND ACTION PLANNING

The information gathering process should help you to identify whether you do want to pursue this new vocation or not. If you decide that a career change is what you want, then you may need to do some in-depth planning. Planning will help you to translate fuzzy goals into concrete actions. It will also identify possible barriers and help you to set realistic timeframes for achieving your new career goals.

Work through the following steps:

1. What **current skills, experience, and qualifications** do you have that would be useful in your new career? Take a sheet of paper and list each of these down the left-hand side.

2. Now think about the **necessary skills, experience and qualifications** that you must have to ensure success in your new career. Write these on the right hand side of the paper.

3. Look at the two lists and identify the **gaps** between them. Draw up a table as follows for each skill gap that you uncover.

Table 10.5

Skill gap	Actions	Timeframe	Resources

4. For the first skill gap, **think about the actions** that you would need to take to address it. Do you, for example, need to pursue a training course?

5. **Think about the timescale for each action.** Can it be accomplished in a period of months or years?

6. Then **think about the resources** that you would need to help you achieve each action. The biggest resource for many people is financial: having enough money to support yourself and your family while perhaps at the same time having to pay tuition fees. However, there are other resources that you may need to draw on, such as the understanding of an employer or the emotional support of a spouse.

7. Do the same for each skill gap. Once you have completed all of the action plans, then take a look at the timescales and combined resource requirements. Given the many actions that you may have to take at once, how realistic are your timescales? Do the resource requirements exceed your current resources? If so, you may need to think about slowing down the pace at which you attempt to change your career in order to deal with practicalities such as having enough money to fund your career transition. The advice on working part-time covered in Chapter 8 might also help to free up some of your time for study or work experience.

8. Finally, look at your completed action plan. Try to estimate how many hours of effort this could involve every week in order to meet those goals. Have you set yourself realistic goals? Many people set goals that are too ambitious – requiring too many activities in too short a period of time – only to end up failing to meet them, feeling very dejected and giving up entirely. I would therefore urge you to set achievable goals over a more reasonable time frame.

A sample action plan

Here is part of a plan that an individual might come up with who is considering re-training to become a journalist:

Table 10.6

Skill gap	Actions	Timeframe	Resources
Qualifications	Look into journalism courses and apply for the most prestigious one	Part-time over the next 12 months, starting in September	Between £1200 and £1600 for course fees
Finance	Pay off credit card debts and start saving for course fees	Before September	
Knowledge of the newspaper industry	Network to meet journalists and editors	ASAP	Ask mother's best friend in media for contacts
Knowledge of working for a newspaper	Investigating opportunities to work for free for a local newspaper	Between September to December	
Lack of a job	Look at weekly media recruitment supplements in national newspapers	Start reading them now: but only apply for a job after March next year	Newspapers

FINAL THOUGHTS

If you are serious about changing careers, then do it. So many people spend their time complaining to friends and family about how unhappy they are at work. But no one likes a moaner, so invest your energy in researching and planning a career switch instead.

If you are still undecided, it may help you to think of what could happen in your future if you stick it out in either an organization that you do not enjoy working for or a job that you can no longer tolerate. Could any of the following statements describe your future?

- 'I'll continue being unhappy and probably regret not having done something.'
- 'I will have a steady job but be bored for the rest of my working life.'
- 'My enthusiasm for work will decline and I'll end up getting fired or made redundant.'

If any of those statements apply to you, then again it suggests that a change of employer or career could be in hand. It will take hard work and application, but I have yet to meet a single person who has embarked on a career change and regretted it. Go on, take your future in your own hands.

11

Achieving what you want through networking

Networking is good for careers, almost irrespective of what your career aims might be. We tend to use networking when we are looking for a new job. Indeed, there is a vast 'hidden market' of jobs that do not get advertised but filled by word of mouth. However, networking is not only useful when you are looking for a new job. Perhaps you want to keep abreast of industry developments to help you stay at the forefront of your field. If you are considering setting up in business on your own, then a strong network of future customers and clients is essential. Neither is networking solely limited to gathering contacts outside your current organization. A strong internal network can act as your eyes and ears, on the look-out for everything from office politics to job opportunities.

Networking is simply a technique for meeting more people and making the best use of the short time that you might have together. Unfortunately, networking can conjure up some rather unpleasant images: talking to people only to see if they can benefit you in some way and flattering them insincerely to get what you want. In reality though, good networking focuses on mutual benefit as opposed to what benefit you can extract from others.

SELF-TEST: MEASURING YOUR NETWORKING SKILLS

Before we discuss how you might network more effectively, this test will help you to establish your current level of networking. Look at the following statements and tick whether you 'agree' or 'disagree' that it describes your attitude and behaviour.

Table 11.1

	Agree	Disagree
1. I always enjoy finding out what other people do		
2. I feel embarrassed asking people for favours		
3. I send Christmas cards to ex-colleagues and other business acquaintances		
4. I call or e-mail ex-colleagues and acquaintances when I am struggling to understand a problem		
5. I don't like to waste time going to conferences		
6. I can't remember the names and family details of all of the members of my team		
7. I cut out articles from the press that I think might interest other colleagues		
8. I prefer to send e-mails or write letters than pick up the telephone		
9. I am quick to return phone calls		
10. I pursue opportunities to work on committees, task forces, and project teams		
11. I like to work problems out on my own		
12. I am happy to ask people for their business cards		
13. I go to social events with people outside of my team		
14. I have lost touch with my ex-bosses		
15. I use the Internet to make contacts with people in my field		
16. I try not to mix my work and my social life		

Estimating your networking skill

Calculate your networking score as follows:

- Award yourself 1 point every time you agreed with any of the following questions – 1, 3, 4, 7, 9, 10, 12, 13 and 15.
- Give yourself another point if you disagreed with questions 2, 5, 6, 8, 11, 14 and 16.

Table 11.2

Your score	Comment
0–5	You don't seem to engage in many networking activities at the moment. Be careful that you don't get overlooked for promotions or other career opportunities. Obviously, read the advice in this chapter. But if you still find the idea of networking a bit nerve-racking, you might want to approach a friend or trusted colleague who you think is a good networker and ask him or her for further tips on how you could do it better.
6–9	You network a little, but if you are interested in raising your profile and identifying career opportunities through relationships with other people, you could do a little more. Look back at the questions on the test. What aren't you doing at the moment?
10–13	You are an above-average networker. But perhaps there are still areas you could improve in. If you network well within your organization, perhaps you need to network more externally – or vice versa.
14–16	You are a natural networker. Just be careful that you don't network so much that you annoy people. People hate feeling that they are being used, so make sure that you are always genuine in your interactions with people and that you offer your time to help them out too.

ANALYSING YOUR NETWORK

When asked to think about their network, most people protest that they do not have one. But the whole point of networking is that it does not matter whether you know anyone 'important' or not to begin with. By networking effectively, you will be able to forge links with people that you had not previously met, building increasingly more useful relationships as you go.

One approach to building a network is by joining your professional association, trade body or union. However, such a strategy will take time to bear fruit if you have a particular goal that you want to achieve from your network. A quicker alternative, then, is to tap into the people that you already know. Start by listing everyone that you know. And by 'everyone', you really do need to begin by writing down a list of every single person whom you currently know or have ever met. This may sound ridiculous, and it is certainly time-consuming, but it is a necessary step. Start with the people that you are currently in contact with. Then think back over previous years to recall even people that you may have lost touch with.

Think about people from all of the different parts of your life. Think about current and past colleagues from other organizations that you have worked in. Then there are customers or clients that you may have worked with: suppliers or professional advisors such as accountants, solicitors and IT support, as well as people whom you may have met at conferences and trade fairs. If you are specifically looking for a new job, then you might even want to look through the phone book for details of headhunters or recruitment consultants.

Do not just stop at your work contacts. Move on to the other spheres of your life. Think about people you were at university or business school with. What about people at local community groups, sports teams or voluntary associations that you belong to?

Critically, you should never leave anyone off the list because you assume that they are not going to be useful, as networks operate in mysterious ways at times. Eventually, if you are diligent with the task, your list should consist of hundreds and hundreds of people.

SETTING YOUR NETWORKING GOALS

The next step is to think about what you want to achieve through networking. There is no point (not to mention not enough time) in getting in touch with every person on your list. So you need to think through:

▪ What are your **objectives** for networking? It may be to do with looking for advice on how to change careers or find a new job. Perhaps you are looking for a business partner to set up a new venture with. Or you might have no particular goal for the moment other than to raise your profile and let others know about your talents.

▪ **Who** can help you achieve your aims? Look back at your list to pick out the individuals who may be able to help you. Either they might have information relevant to your objectives, or perhaps you think they are more likely to know someone who could be able to help.

PREPARING TO NETWORK

When networking, the ideal situation is to get in touch by telephoning, with the intention of setting up a short face-to-face meeting. Obviously, not everyone has the time to meet you in person. However, it is much easier to build a rapport with individuals and get them to lower their guard than if you are merely talking on the telephone.

When thinking about how to approach someone, it may help you to think about the six 'I's of networking.

1   Identification

Initially you may be speaking to people that you know, but the whole point of networking is that you will soon be speaking to people you have never spoken to before. So you need to 'identify' yourself to these people who do not know you by explaining who you are and why you are getting in touch. So think about the five or six sentences that you are going to use to explain the purpose of your telephone call. In a world of busy people, first impressions are critical. So be succinct and to the point.

Some people find it useful to write down a script, almost word for word. As you progress with your telephone calls and meetings, you can eliminate parts of your script that do not seem to work very well and incorporate better words and phrases.

2   Ice breaking

Think about what you and the contact may have in common. Some contacts like a bit of personal chit-chat before getting to the nub of the conversation. It may therefore help you to have one or two topics of conversation that you could discuss for a few minutes.

Some people worry that they have nothing in common with a potential contact. However, the reality is that we all have families and personal relationships. We all eat and drink and take the occasional holiday. Most importantly of all, we would all like more from our work: whether it is promotions, more respect, more pay, having to work less hard for the same amount of money or whatever. If you are desperate, then there are always topics such as the weather and traffic. Such topics may help the contact to warm to you and perhaps give you a little more time and consideration than they otherwise might.

3   Information gathering

You need to think of the questions you are going to ask. If you are looking for particular insights from contacts, then it may help you to write down the questions that you would like to ask ahead of time.

Brainstorm a list of potential questions, but then group them according to priority. If a contact is short on time, you do not want to waste the few minutes that you have together. Always begin by asking the most important questions.

4   Introductions

The whole point of networking is to be able to approach people that you do not personally know. In fact, the person you first ring will rarely have the information you are seeking. So always try to get at least one name and number from each contact you speak to.

Many contacts will initially say, 'I don't think I can think of anyone who can help you with that.' However, the reality is that many people could have useful contacts if only they took a few moments to think about it. So politely suggest that any kind of suggestion, advice or contact that they might be able to come up with could be useful. Stress also that you are willing to pursue any leads at all – no matter how remote – because you realize that the networking process can be a lengthy one.

However, if they insist that they do not know anyone then do not press the issue, as you do not want to establish a reputation that would make other people avoid you rather than be receptive to your efforts to make contact with them.

5   Interview notes

Taking notes will be vital if you want to keep track of your networking. What you take down is up to you, but good notes will ensure that you do not harass an individual by getting in touch with them twice by mistake. In addition, networking for information is like constructing a jigsaw puzzle, each individual comment may not seem terribly useful until it is all assembled at some later date.

6   Impression

Remember that networking is not just about you, it is about establishing a mutual benefit wherever possible. The benefit may be as little as giving the other person your respect for their industry knowledge and your sincere thanks for their time. Or it could be that you will keep them informed as to your progress in getting a new job, setting up a new company and so on.

MAINTAINING YOUR NETWORK

Networking is a powerful technique for meeting more people, gathering information and raising your profile. But it is also time-consuming. So now that you have invested all that time and effort into making these new contacts, you should aim to maintain the size and diversity of your network.

What you do to maintain your network is up to you. It depends on the nature of the relationship you have with each individual contact. For example, it may be appropriate to forward humorous e-mails to a close friend of a friend. For others it might be a dignified Christmas card or a personalized letter informing them about a change in your work details.

As time passes, some contacts will move on, but at the same time you should meet new contacts. You should also get a better sense of the individuals you want to spend more time on, those that seem to have an interest in seeking mutual benefit with you. Occasionally, you may find yourself having to invest in a focused burst of intensive networking; at other times you may find that you do not need to get in touch with them for a long period of time. But do keep hold of that list, as you can never predict when you might need the answer to a question that you cannot answer for yourself.

12

Figuring out your next employer

It is a great feeling to be offered a job. Whether you networked your way into it, got headhunted, or went through the good old-fashioned route of applying to a job advertisement, you should congratulate yourself. The advice in Chapter 9 should have helped you to negotiate a good package, so it may seem like an offer that you cannot refuse.

But you CAN refuse the offer. In fact, you should put off making a decision for a few days to give yourself some time to think it through. Before you accept the offer, you need to be confident that it is right for you. In particular, you need to be positive that you can answer 'yes' to the following two questions:

1. Am I certain that I will enjoy all of the aspects of this job?
2. Will this job help me to achieve my long-term career aims?

The advice and questions in this chapter should help you to make up your mind. When a business is thinking about acquiring another company, it will engage in a process of due diligence: collecting facts, figures and opinions about the potential target. In particular, due diligence is often about ensuring that there are no nasty surprises should the deal go through. Similarly, when making a decision whether to accept an offer or not, investing just a few days of cautious thought and judicious investigation might help you to avoid years of grief in the wrong job.

TWENTY QUESTIONS TO ASK

Looking at promotional literature or information on a Web site is not going to tell you anything; organizations frequently do not practise what they preach. Your only option is to spend some time talking to your prospective employer.

The interview process itself is rarely the best time to ask truly probing questions about your potential employer. Finding good questions to ask during interviews is a fine balance between gathering information and creating the right impression. However, with an offer on the table, you will never have a better opportunity to ask some really probing questions. Here are just 20 questions (and a few supplementary questions) that you might like to choose from. Broadly, they fall into four categories:

Pay and reward

1. How will my performance be measured?
2. How will my targets be set? And how much say will I have in setting them?
3. Who are the key decision-makers that I will need to get along with? And how would you describe each of them?
4. How regularly will my pay be reviewed? And when will be my first review?

5. How much of my bonus is guaranteed? And how much of it is dependent on performance?

Doing the job

6. Be honest with me, what do you really think of the members of the team that I would be running or working with?

7. What do you see as the immediate challenges for me if I were to be given the job?

8. When was the last company restructuring? And how did it affect this department?

9. How is the organization performing? What do staff and shareholders think of the company's performance?

10. Are there any big changes or restructuring planned for the near future?

11. So what exactly happened to the previous job holder?

Culture

12. How would you describe the culture of the organization?

13. What is the best thing about working for this organization?

14. I promise that I won't mention it to anyone, but just between you and me, what frustrates you most about working here?

15. Would you describe this as a political organization? And if so, why?

16. How much inter-departmental rivalry is there in the company?

17. How much do people socialize together outside of work? What was the last social event that you went to?

The future

18. What training and development is given to employees?

19. What opportunities are there for promotion?

20. Could you tell me about the sorts of people who have failed here? What was it they did or didn't do that made them unsuccessful?

MEETING THE TEAM

The 20 questions above can unearth lots of interesting information about the potential employer. But an employer is likely to put forward only its most acceptable employees for you to meet. Typically, they might provide a select group of socially skilled and presentable managers, and these individuals are likely to talk about only certain aspects of the culture: the brand that they would *like* to present to potential recruits. However, we all know that what *really* goes on within an organization is not always fairly represented. If you really want to know what life in the organization is like, though, you should try to meet some of the people that you would end up working with.

Ask if you can spend some time – perhaps only a half-day – speaking to peers who might work with you, or members of any team that might be reporting to you. Not all of the 20 questions will be appropriate, but most of the ones from questions 6 to 20 should be okay. If at all possible, ask to meet people on a one-to-one basis as well as over an informal event such as lunch, a drink in a local pub, or dinner. People who might be guarded in a work setting may be more revealing in a different setting.

But meeting the team is not just about your prospective colleagues. Given that many organizations try to form partnerships with their customers and clients – and even their suppliers – you could argue that these constitute part of the wider team. Asking if it would be possible for you to meet a few of these external partners could give you an invaluable picture of the reputation of the organization.

Your prospective employer might be a bit hesitant to put you in a customer-facing situation. Realistically, a potential employer is not going to give you such an opportunity unless you are being considered for either a management role or a job in the £30,000+ salary bracket. However, if you explain that you really like the people you have met within the organization, but want a greater understanding of the organization's market and customers before you can make up your mind, your potential employer might relent.

OPENING YOUR EYES AND EARS

Another valuable source of information is what you can see and hear around you when you wander through the employer's premises. Think about the following issues and what you may be looking for in an employer:

- Is the office laid out in an open plan or not? Is 'hot desking' a feature of the workplace?
- How does the building strike you? Is it glamorous or self-satisfied, homely or run-down?
- What do you think of the location of where you will be working? Is it a 'good' area of town? What would your journey to work be like?
- How up-to-date are the IT systems and office technology? Would computer problems cause you difficulties later on?
- How are people dressed? Is there a formal or casual dress code?
- What do the workspaces look like? Are they cluttered and disorganized or obsessively tidy? Are personal items allowed to be displayed on the work surfaces?

None of the above questions have right or wrong, better or worse answers. What suits most people may not suit you. For example, you may enjoy an informal, dress-down, working environment where employees are allowed to leave evidence of their existence all around their desk. Or perhaps you feel offended by the waste of money that is the employer's glitzy steel and glass office location in the centre of town. You need to choose.

MAKING A DECISION

At the start of this chapter, I raised two questions that you need to be able to answer to your personal satisfaction:

1.   Am I certain that I will enjoy all of the aspects of this job?
2.   Will this job help me to achieve my long-term career aims?

Now that you have collected some evidence by interviewing your prospective employer, meeting your potential colleagues, and soaking up the atmosphere, you should be able to make a decision.

You should now have a good sense of whether you would enjoy working in the company. Did you find your potential colleagues pleasant? Would you find your personal objectives and targets acceptable? You may also want to refer back to the likes and dislikes exercise at the start of Chapter 10. Is this organization's culture right for you?

In answering the second question, though, do refer back to the notes that you should have taken in working through Chapter 1. The whole purpose of that first chapter was to help you decide on what your long-term career aims should be. If what you have seen and heard from your employer about the sort of work you would be doing does not fit in with those career aims, then you must really ask yourself whether this job is right for you.

Perhaps, if it does help you to advance slightly towards your career goal, it could be good enough. On the other hand, are there other jobs out there that could help you take a bigger step towards your ultimate career goal?

I'm afraid that I cannot help you any further. The final decision is up to you. Good luck!

Conclusion

There is a lot of material covered in this book. If you raced through it, then you are not making the most of the book. I will mention again that the way to get the most out of this book is to take it slowly. Read a bit of a chapter, complete a self-test questionnaire, and maybe set the book aside to think about your future. Where are you now? And where would you like to be in a year, two years, five years or ten years?

You may want to skip some chapters for the moment because they just do not seem relevant to your current situation, and that's fine. But keep the book with you, as you might discover that the issue crops up later on in your career, perhaps as you climb the career ladder or move onto new jobs. The idea of job-sharing may be completely alien to you at this moment in time, but it could become increasingly attractive later on in life. Or you may need to gain considerably more experience of working for other people before you can realistically decide to set up in business on your own.

Other issues are bound to crop up again and again, perhaps in a different form each time. If you are thinking about taking a new job, then you will need to figure out each potential employer in turn. Once you are there, you will need to build solid relationships with all of your colleagues, thinking about the best way to influence and persuade them, while at the same time keeping an eye out for office politics. Each different employer is also likely to have unique methods of running appraisals, promotion interviews and other organizational procedures. Work is a merry-go-round, and hopefully this book will help you to avoid getting dizzy.

Finally, I sincerely hope that you find this book useful. I have tried to gather together a number of diverse issues from my work in consulting with client organizations. E-mail me on robyeung@robyeung.freeserve.co.uk or write to me c/o the publisher, Kogan Page, to let me know of your successes and disasters.

Best of luck.

Index